Open for Debate

Free Trade

Open for Debate
Free Trade

Kathiann M. Kowalski

Marshall Cavendish
Benchmark
New York

This book is dedicated to my daughter,
Laura Kathryn Meissner.

The author gratefully thanks the following people
for sharing their insights and comments:
Sarah Anderson and John Cavanagh
at the Institute for Policy Studies,
Robin Broad at The American University,
Pradip Kamat at Indus International Inc.,
Mehrene Larudee at DePaul University,
Laura K. Meissner at The SEEP Network,
Michael Meissner, Pietra Rivoli at Georgetown University,
and Mark Weisbrot at the Center for
Economic and Policy Research.

Marshall Cavendish Benchmark
99 White Plains Road
Tarrytown, NY 10591-9001
www.marshallcavendish.us

Library of Congress Cataloging-in-Publication Data
Kowalski, Kathiann M., 1955–
Free trade / by Kathiann M. Kowalski.
p. cm.
Summary: "Discusses the history of international trade, and outlines the
arguments of those both for and against free trade, including the effects on
world economies, the labor force, and the environment"
—Provided by publisher.
Includes bibliographical references and index.
ISBN-13: 978-0-7614-2575-5
1. Free trade. 2. International trade—History. 3. International
economic integration—History. 4. Globalization—Economic aspects—History.
I. Title.
HF1713.K675 2006
382'.71—dc22
2006019234

Photo research by Lindsay Aveilhe and Linda Sykes
Linda Sykes Photo Research, Hilton Head, SC

Amit Bhargava/Corbis: cover, 1, 5; AP/World Wide Photos: 6; Bobby Yip/Reuters/
Corbis: 16; Bob Krist/Corbis: 18; ©Topkapi Palace Museum, Istanbul, Turkey/
Giraudon/The Bridgeman Art Library: 25; Bettmann/Corbis: 27; AFP/Getty Images:
35; ©Bibliotheque Nationale, Paris, France/ Lauros /Giraudon/The Bridgeman Art
Library: 40; Fayaz Kabli/Reuters/Corbis: 49; AP/World Wide Photos: 68; AP/World
Wide Photos: 71; Reuters/Corbis: 81; Hagerty Parick/Corbis Sygma: 87;
Kapoor Baldev/Sygma/Corbis: 101.

Publisher: Michelle Bisson
Art Director: Anahid Hamparian
Series Designer: Sonia Chaghatzbanian

Printed in China

1 3 5 6 4 2

Contents

CONTAINERS AT A CHINESE DOCKYARD AWAIT SHIPMENT OVERSEAS.
CHINESE EXPORTS TO THE UNITED STATES HAVE GROWN BY LEAPS

1
What's the Big Deal?
The Fuss over
Free Trade

When the World Trade Organization (WTO) met in December 2005, the gathering should have been the crowning point in a four-year round of talks among the group's 149 member countries. Approximately 6,000 representatives gathered in Hong Kong. Their goal—and the overall goal of the WTO—was to promote free trade.

Since the end of World War II, the free trade movement has sought to lower trade barriers between countries. Industrialized nations dropped tariffs (import taxes) on manufactured goods from an average of 40 percent to approximately 4 percent. The movement lowered other restrictions on trade too.

Meanwhile, technological advances in transportation and communication have made it practical for many companies to do business on a global scale. The volume of international trade has skyrocketed to approximately $9 trillion worth of global exports. The WTO representatives at the Hong Kong meeting hoped to make more progress on lowering trade barriers, including those on agricultural products.

Just as the WTO meeting was about to begin, however, thousands more people took to Hong Kong's streets in protest. Among them were many South Korean farmers, who felt that rice imports into their country were destroying their livelihood. Other protesters complained that the WTO put the interests of wealthy corporations before those of poor people, workers, and consumers.

Many protesters behaved peacefully. Unfortunately, some violent clashes and riots broke out. Protesters attacked police with bamboo sticks, metal rods, and rocks. Police battled back with batons and tear gas, arresting over 900 people. Almost 100 individuals suffered physical injuries.

The Hong Kong protests disappointed the meeting's organizers. However, the protests were no huge surprise. At the 2003 WTO meetings in Cancun, Mexico, a protesting South Korean farmer killed himself with a knife. Those meetings ended in a stalemate after representatives from twenty-one poor nations walked out because of disagreements between poor and wealthy nations.

Indeed, mass protests took center stage when the WTO met in Seattle in 1999. Approximately 50,000 individuals from different groups gathered there to protest different aspects of the WTO and the free trade movement. Many saw themselves as advocates for the world's poor people. Thousands were environmentalists, worried about conservation and pollution. Thousands of union members attended too. They wanted better working conditions for foreign laborers. Many of them also worried about their own job security in the United States.

The protesting groups came from many backgrounds and had different reasons for coming. Yet most agreed with the cry voiced at one of the week's rallies by United

Steelworkers of America president George Becker: "Who the hell asked our leaders to give us the WTO?"

The protests disrupted the WTO gathering, which ended with no clear agreements or compromises. Meanwhile, police had arrested hundreds of people. And the city of Seattle faced millions of dollars in damage from riots and looting.

International Trade: A Big Deal

As the stormy protests against the WTO show, the topic of free trade triggers passionate feelings. At the same time, international trade is big business. Free trade champions say the United States has already been a big winner. For most of the time since World War II, the United States has been the world's largest trading nation. In 2004, for example, American importers and exporters were parties to about one-sixth of the total world trade in goods and nearly one-fifth of the total world trade in services. Because of international trade agreements, the Office of the U.S. Trade Representative reports, the average family enjoys better quality products, more consumer choices, and savings between $1,300 and $2,000 each year.

What does America's leading trade position mean in dollars? In 2005, about $4.3 trillion of goods, services, and investment income and payments came into or went out of the United States. Exports of goods came to almost $894 billion—an increase of 78 percent since 1994. Exports of services totaled $380 billion—an increase of 90 percent since 1994. Generally, services are tasks that people do. Goods are tangible products or, as *The Economist* has put it, "things you can drop on your toe."

At the same time, America was importing more goods and services than ever. The $1.7 trillion worth of goods imported during 2005 represented a 150 percent increase over the value of goods imported in 1994. The $323 billion worth of services imported during 2005 was 143 percent higher than 1994 levels. All told, the United States imported over $700 million more in goods and services than it exported. Can this continue without seriously harming the United States' overall economic health? The current trade imbalance is one issue in the debate over trade policy.

Disagreements about free trade also deal with the broader issue of globalization. Simply stated, globalization is the increasing trend towards trade and business taking place across political borders. Increasingly, companies are no longer limited to any nation's boundaries. A company may have its worldwide headquarters in one nation yet have operations around the world.

For free trade champions, globalization represents the increasing interdependence among the world's national economies. It reflects a growing role for more countries in the realm of international trade and economics. And it presents the promise of potential economic growth that could lift millions of people out of poverty, especially in developing nations.

For free trade critics, however, globalization reflects the growing dominance of multinational corporations. Those corporate interests often have substantial sway over how governments act. As a result, critics say, the free trade movement often promotes the interests of large corporations at the expense of the world's poor people, its workers, and the environment. While global trade increases and corporations reap huge profits, the number of poor people in Africa, Latin America, and other regions has risen.

Human rights issues also come up in the debate. Boycotts and trade restrictions worked with other international pressure to get South Africa to end its racist apartheid policies in 1993. The United States has long had an embargo, or prohibition, against any trade with Cuba because of the communist regime there. As another example, widespread violence and human rights violations led the United States to ban imports from Burma (also called Myanmar) in 2003.

Meanwhile, trade is booming with countries like China, which is accused of oppressing its people in various ways. Critics feel that countries accused of human rights violations should not get to trade with other countries on an even footing. Free trade supporters like the Cato Institute feel it is best to let the market work on its own. In time, they say, freer trade and economic well-being will lead to better protection of human rights.

Other aspects of the free trade debate focus on how international commerce affects America's job market. The United States and other wealthy nations generally have higher wages and better standards of living than developing countries. As import barriers drop, trade policies can lead companies to shift jobs elsewhere. In other words, instead of making a product or providing a service in the United States, a company may find it easier and cheaper to send the work abroad. Workers thus wind up in competition with laborers around the world.

Free trade critics argue that the movement drags down wages and worker standards in a worldwide "race to the bottom." Millions of jobs are at stake. Meanwhile, critics say, free trade policies promote the exploitation of cheap labor in foreign sweatshops.

Free trade supporters say fair competition leads to shifts in jobs making goods or providing services. In other words, it is part of the market at work, and it leads to better products and greater efficiency. Plus, supporters say, as poor countries earn more from exports, market and social forces can improve the plight of their workers.

The free trade debate involves the environment, too. Environmental regulations vary from country to country. Should products made in heavily polluting nations compete on the same basis as those made in environmentally responsible ways? Do free trade policies discourage countries from taking necessary measures to protect our planet? If so, can the world really afford the environmental costs of such economic progress?

Another worry is whether America relies too much on imports. The United States already depends on foreign suppliers for most of its petroleum, and much of that oil comes from politically unstable areas. Because of this, presidents from Jimmy Carter to George W. Bush have called on America to take steps to reduce its dependency on foreign oil.

Other products are equally vital to America's security and economic well being. The defense industry, for example, requires a reliable source of steel. Free trade critics say America should not lose the ability to provide for its own needs. It should not have to depend on the rest of the world.

Despite criticisms, imports continue to grow, and countries keep negotiating for lower trade barriers. It sometimes seems as if globalization and the move for free trade are going ahead, no matter what. Meanwhile, critics continue to voice their objections. Later chapters explore these issues in detail.

Playing Fairly

Questions about fair play and legitimate competition come up as well. Nations use a variety of policies to bolster and promote their economies, sometimes at the expense of other countries. Even President George W. Bush, one of America's biggest champions of free trade, qualifies his position by calling for a "level playing field."

We've signed a lot of free trade agreements, and at the same time we've done so, we've said to

countries, listen, just treat us the way we treat you. That's all we ask. Level the playing field. There is no doubt in my mind, American farmers and entrepreneurs and business people and . . . employees can compete with anybody, any time, anywhere, so long as the rules are fair.

Whether there is a level playing field affects how well the market can operate. Most economists base arguments in favor of free trade on the theory of comparative advantage. As discussed later, the theory of comparative advantage holds that countries maximize their wealth by concentrating on things they do better relative to other nations, and buying other products through trade. In other words, even if a country can make a wide range of products more efficiently than others, it should focus on where it is most efficient and import other things.

Tariffs and other barriers to trade distort the market, the theory says. In other words, they affect price and alter how buyers and sellers behave. Suppose, for example, that an importer must pay $2 in tariffs on a toy it imports for $10. The importer will probably add that $2 to the price charged to consumers. The import might then be more expensive for consumers to buy than similar toys made in the United States.

Free trade champions say trade barriers lead to inefficiency. In the toy example, domestic producers don't have to compete as hard with the foreign producers. As a result, consumers pay more, and the country benefits less overall than it would if there were no trade restrictions.

Some barriers to trade are open and obvious. Others are more disguised. Tariffs are a classic and obvious way for countries to protect their own industries from foreign competition.

The import tax goes to the government. However, someone must pay that added cost. To cover it, importers usually increase the price they charge the consumer. This makes imported products less attractive, price-wise, than domestic ones.

Quotas also control imports. A quota limits how much of a certain product can come in each year from one or more countries. Quotas protect against foreign suppliers flooding the market with cheap imports when their own economies could not react quickly to such change. However, free trade supporters say, quotas shield domestic producers from competition.

For example, the United States and other countries have long set quotas on imported textiles and clothing. As a result of a WTO agreement, countries began lifting some of those restrictions in 2005. However, some restrictions will stay in place for the next several years, especially for Chinese clothing and fabrics.

Regulatory standards come into play too. People generally agree that nations ought to be able to control the quality of products sold in their country. Among other things, standards can protect public health and the environment, as well as consumer rights. In the United States, for example, pollution control equipment for motor vehicles must meet various requirements. As another example, young children's toys must meet standards meant to protect against the risk of choking on small parts.

Sometimes, however, nations' standards keep other countries' products out. Suppose that one nation's laws required all automobile parts sold in the country to have a particular certification of quality. Then suppose that the only practical way to get that certification was if the parts were actually made within that country. Car buyers would want to know that they could readily get replacement parts when needed. Unless domestic auto parts would work in the car, the certification requirement could limit the market for imported cars.

As another example, suppose that a country had a rule

about the minimum size for selling pineapples. If pineapples grown in another area of the world were generally smaller, they could not enter the market, even if they were just as tasty. The nation imposing the standard might argue that the regulation protects consumers from unwittingly buying fruit that has too much waste. Countries kept out of the market could say that the standard insulates the domestic growers from competition.

Dumping is another ploy countries sometimes use. Dumping occurs when a country sells its product to foreign buyers for substantially less than cost. Even if the exporting country has a short-term loss, the lower prices could drive competition away. That would increase the exporting country's market share.

Subsidies also raise questions about fair play. Subsidies provide financial or other help to an industry. Producers at home argue that economic ruin could result without the government's help. Other countries may say it is unfair competition when subsidies make one country's product far cheaper than their own products.

American farmers get various subsidies. Sometimes the government pays farmers to grow certain crops. Sometimes it guarantees extra income if market prices fall below set levels. The government sometimes promises to purchase certain amounts of products, or it promotes sales, as in the federal program for milk and cheese in schools. Tax breaks and cheap or free support services act as subsidies too.

Disagreements about farm subsidies remained a major problem at the 2005 WTO talks in Hong Kong. Developing countries wanted to eliminate subsidies, so their farmers could compete in the world market. European Union countries with heavy farm subsidies wanted to protect their own farmers. Farm subsidies remain on the WTO's agenda.

Financial policies also affect international trade. Most

PROTESTERS VOICED A VARIETY OF OBJECTIONS TO THE WORLD TRADE ORGANIZATION AT THE ORGANIZATION'S 2005 CONFERENCE IN HONG KONG.

countries let their currencies "float." In other words, the value relative to other countries' money goes up or down, depending on changes in the world market. For example, a dollar may be worth so many Euros or yen today, but a different amount tomorrow, next month, or next year. However, there are exceptions.

China, for example, controls how much its yuan, the "people's currency," is worth in American dollars. Changes in exchange rates can cause one country's products to be a better buy than another's. When market forces determine the rate, that's one thing. If a country consistently sets its currency's value lower than the market, however, its exports appear cheaper to foreign buyers.

Economist Peter Morici at the University of Maryland claims that China's stance has given it an unfair trade advantage worth approximately one-third of the value of its exports.

The U. S. government has urged China to relax regulation of its currency rates. From China's standpoint, however, suddenly lifting all control over the yuan's value could cause havoc in the country's economy and financial markets. In 2006, the country finally let the yuan's value grow to slightly less than eight yuan per dollar. Yet China was still on track that year for a $150 billion surplus in its balance of trade from the sale of goods.

Taking Sides

Free trade's champions and critics do not line up neatly along the political spectrum. Politically conservative groups like the Cato Institute claim that free trade is good for America. Yet conservative commentator Patrick Buchanan argues that free trade jeopardizes America's sovereignty—its right to rule itself and determine its own destiny. CNN financial analyst Lou Dobbs, a longtime Republican, argues that corporate greed fuels the push for free trade and globalization, to the detriment of America and its workers.

On the more liberal end, free trade critics include labor groups like the AFL-CIO (American Federation of Labor–Congress of Industrial Organizations) and the International Labor Organization, environmental groups like Greenpeace, and the Economic Policy Institute. Yet Harvard professor Jeffrey Sachs has argued that Democrats ought to back free trade as a way to promote social and economic welfare. And while President Bill Clinton was more liberal than his successor, President George W. Bush, both have been cheerleaders for free trade.

Differences between theory and reality complicate

GENERAL MOTORS SHUT DOWN THIS MANUFACTURING PLANT IN FLINT, MICHIGAN, DURING THE 1980s.

matters as well. Economists do not always agree on how theories should work. Moreover, the real world never behaves exactly the way theories say it should. Buyers and sellers do not always do what economists predict. Capital, or investment money, does not move as easily as theories assume it does. Workers cannot always switch directly from one job to another, either.

Political, social, and environmental concerns all complicate the picture. Something might be "good" in the short term for maximizing a nation's gross domestic product (GDP)—a measure of how much a country makes or earns in a year. However, that move might cause longer-term environmental harm, or it might have other adverse political or social consequences.

Beyond all this, trade policy does not affect everyone the same way. A particular action might open up foreign markets for particular industries. Greater demand can lead to higher profits and more job openings in those industries. Workers' added buying power could then help stimulate other parts of the economy.

However, the same move could subject other industries to more intense foreign competition. Companies in those industries would see profits shrink and may wind up laying off workers. Some companies may even go out of business.

Thus, even if the overall net effect of a trade policy increases a country's GDP, the policy's effects are uneven. Some people and industries may win big. Others may suffer substantially. Mehrene Larudee at DePaul University explains:

> **When an economist says that a country benefits from opening up trade, this means, quite simply, that the winners gain more than the losers lose, and therefore could, in principle, pay the losers enough to completely compensate them for their losses, and still have money left over.**

As a practical matter, that compensation usually does not get paid. Nonetheless, the net result for the country as a whole is still positive.

On a theoretical level, shifts in international trade patterns change the structure of countries' economies. Indeed, the United States' economy is never static and is constantly changing. Some sectors grow, while others shrink. Those changes almost always displace workers in some fields. Over time, the economy tends to adjust, and labor shifts to accommodate the demands of the market.

Those moves never take place simultaneously, however. Even in the best of cases, workers often need training

Who Made Your T-Shirt?

At a college rally, one speaker sought to raise the crowd's awareness about how laborers are often exploited in the name of global trade. To hammer her point home, she challenged the crowd, "Who made your T-shirt?" Intrigued by the question, Georgetown professor Pietra Rivoli decided to find out. The result was *The Travels of a T-Shirt in the Global Economy: An Economist Examines the Markets, Power, and Politics of World Trade*.

Rivoli bought a $5.99 parrot T-shirt labeled "Made in China" and traced its history. Large Texas farms grow cotton, which gets shipped to China and other countries around the world. Factories in China spin and knit cotton into fabric and sew it into T-shirts. A Florida company imported Rivoli's shirt and screen-printed the parrot design. After Rivoli tires of her shirt, its life might continue elsewhere. Secondhand T-shirts are very popular in Africa.

Despite T-shirts' extensive travels, very little real free trade takes place, says Rivoli. Texas farmers get subsidies and other government help that gives them an edge over growers in other countries. The Chinese government owns or controls most businesses, maintains rigid control over its currency, and imposes substantial restrictions on workers. Those factors keep costs low and help make China's exports attractive to foreign buyers. Once the shirts were made, import quotas restricted how many shirts could come into the United States and other countries. Even in the African resale market, where there was the most competition, there were still tariffs and other restrictions.

"Free trade is an ideal that is never really achieved in practice," explains Rivoli. The theory behind free trade is that free and open competition will lead to the greatest good for everyone. But competition does not take place on a level playing field. Tariffs, quotas, subsidies, financial policies, and controlled labor markets all affect products' attractiveness in the global marketplace.

Remember that while global trade is much more open than it was sixty years ago, it is still a long way from the ideal of free trade. Also keep in mind that issues involving trade are often more complex than they seem. Rivoli found this out when she tried to answer the "simple" question, "Who made your T-shirt?"

to qualify for jobs in growing industries. In the worst cases, other fields may not have enough good jobs available to absorb workers from other industries. The impacts on displaced workers are both substantial and very personal.

Because displaced workers are voters, politicians worry about them and listen to their complaints. Indeed, significant downturns for a particular industry can have broad impacts at the local and state levels. At the national level, policy makers should also help the country's economy as a whole. Often they walk a delicate tightrope, trying to stay in line with party leaders' policies, while avoiding major upsets for the voters back home. At the same time, many politicians rely on campaign contributions from multinational companies that profit from international trade.

Thus, the free trade movement is not a matter of "deal or no deal." International trade has grown substantially in recent decades, and that trend is likely to continue. The real questions focus on how that will happen.

2
Let's Make a Deal: International Trade in History

International trade has gone on for thousands of years. Approximately 3,000 years ago, the ancient Phoenicians exported an unusual reddish-purple cloth, colored from shellfish found in their Middle Eastern homeland. Phoenician merchants also exported wine, olive oil, and cedar timber from their homeland. In return, they brought back precious metals and other goods from foreign lands.

The ancient Greeks and Romans used their vast empires for trade. Their dealings reached beyond their boundaries too. Ancient Roman goods would travel through the Mediterranean to Egypt. From there, they went overland to Red Sea ports and then sailed on ships bound for India. On the return trip, the ships brought back spices and other goods from India.

Meanwhile, caravans along the Silk Road carried precious metals, gems, glass, and other goods to lands in the Far East. Their return trips brought back silks from China, as well as ceramics, lacquerware, iron, and other goods. Deals along the way bought spices and other valuable commodities.

The Silk Road continued as a vital trade route even after the Roman Empire collapsed. By 1000 C.E. Arab merchants dominated trade along the route. By the late thirteenth century, Europeans began traveling along the Silk Road as well. Probably the most famous traveler was Marco Polo (1254–1324), who traveled throughout China and was well known to the Mongol leader, Kublai Khan (1215–1294).

Marco Polo's writings captured Europeans' imagination. People desired to travel and explore new lands. And they loved the wonderful goods that trade could bring from China, India, and other Asian lands. The trip by land was long and difficult, and there were limits to how much traders could carry back. Also, Arabs controlled the routes and often charged travelers for access.

By the early fifteenth century, China and India were producing about three-fourths of the world's GDP. Europeans could not get enough of their wares and soon began seeking other ways to get to the Far East for trade. Portugal's Bartholomew Diaz (c.1450–1500) succeeded in sailing around Africa's Cape of Good Hope in 1488. That opened the way for ships to sail further east to Asia, which Vasco da Gama (c.1469–1524) did by landing on India's west coast in 1498. "For Christ and spices!" shouted his crew when they landed.

Meanwhile, Christopher Columbus had persuaded the Spanish government to fund his quest to sail west. While he did not make it to either India or China, Columbus landed in North America in 1492. With Europeans traveling the continents, a worldwide wave of colonization began.

Europe Expands Its Reach

From the fifteenth century until World War I in the twentieth century, Europe extended its grasp on the global econ-

CHINESE CERAMICS WERE JUST ONE OF MANY FINE GOODS TRANS-
PORTED ALONG THE SILK ROAD. THIS ORIGINAL PAINTED SILK ARTWORK
DATES BACK TO THE FIFTEENTH CENTURY.

omy. Spain, France, and other countries used their political and military might to colonize vast areas of Africa, North America, and South America, and they took advantage of the riches of those lands. Along Africa's west coast, for example, Europeans helped themselves to gold and ivory. They also profited from an intercontinental slave trade that plundered Africa's population for hundreds of years.

Not content with their existing colonial empires, Europe's countries competed vigorously with each other over foreign lands, and wars broke out. In large part, the desire to control sources of raw materials fueled those rivalries. Colonies also provided captive markets for manufactured goods from the ruling country.

Throughout this era, international commerce thrived. Yet it was anything but free trade. During the seventeenth century, for example, British laws let Virginia farmers export tobacco only to England. Colonial farmers had to accept the price they were offered. They could not seek a higher price from other countries in the international market.

As colonial farmers made less than they would have earned with free competition, disparities between rich and poor people grew. The colonial government's failure to protect farmers from attacks by Native Americans was the spark that triggered Bacon's Rebellion at Jamestown in 1676. Yet trade restrictions also played a part in that uprising. The English government squashed the revolt, yet it kept using its colonies as captive markets.

Nearly one hundred years later, Great Britain again incurred Americans' anger by passing the Tea Act of 1773. At first glance, the law lowered the price of tea by letting the East India Company sell to the colonists without middlemen. However, the law also gave that company a monopoly. Rather than let England eliminate all competition, angry colonists dumped hundreds of cases of tea into the

Protests by the American colonists during the Boston Tea Party in 1773 were a response to restrictive trade policies imposed by Great Britain.

harbor during the Boston Tea Party. The incident was just one of many that led to America eventually declaring its independence from Great Britain.

As a young country, the United States quickly began trading with other countries. It also aimed to help its domestic industries grow. Among other things, the government imposed protective tariffs on manufactured goods brought in from other countries. While the government earned some revenue from those taxes, their chief effect was to raise the price consumers paid for imported goods. By comparison, consumers paid less for textiles and other items manufactured at home. The tariff protected the country's new industries from foreign competition. Meanwhile, however, consumers had to pay more for manufactured goods.

The protective tariffs added to tensions between the North and South. During the nineteenth century, manufacturing of textiles and other items was based primarily in the northern states. Those states thus enjoyed whatever benefits were to be had from the protective tariffs. In contrast, people in the South had to pay higher prices for manufactured goods, without any direct benefit. They felt as if they were subsidizing the North's rapid economic growth. While slavery was the primary issue that led to the Civil War, this economic tension fueled rivalry between the South and North.

The Industrial Revolution took place throughout the eighteenth and nineteenth centuries in Europe and the United States. Factory machines did most of the manufacturing work that skilled craftspeople had previously done by hand or with simple machines in cottage industries. The growth of factories and manufacturing caused many people to move from rural areas to cities in search of jobs. Major changes were under way in society.

The United States was growing as a nation and a new economic power. Yet Great Britain still dominated international trade through most of the nineteenth century. Besides having had a head start in manufacturing, it still had a vast colonial empire that supported it economically.

In 1846, Great Britain repealed its Corn Laws, which were a set of strict import restrictions. Economic historians see that move as the point when Britain's economy switched from being mostly agricultural to primarily industrial. Free trade champions also see the move as acceptance of the theory of comparative advantage, insofar as the country would concentrate on what it did best—manufacturing—and import other items, like food, with few or no restrictions. This point is debatable, since Great Britain did not drop all its tariffs. It also continued to reap wealth from its colonies in Africa, Asia, and elsewhere, while controlling the prices it paid for their goods.

International trade kept growing as the twentieth century began. With its vast empire and high degree of industrialization, Great Britain led the pack as the world's largest trader. But countries still had significant restrictions and imposed tariffs on imports. The world had a lot of international trade, but it was not free trade.

Then, amid mounting political tensions, an assassin killed Austria's Archduke Francis Ferdinand. That murder served as the spark that set off World War I in 1914. International trade dropped off dramatically.

Isolation and Depression

After World War I, even Europe's victorious countries faced steep problems in getting their economies back on track. And harsh treaty terms crippled the economies of the losing countries, especially Germany. Meanwhile, across the Atlantic Ocean, the United States took an isolationist stance and withdrew from the international political arena as much as possible.

A general sense of prosperity swept through America

during the "Roaring Twenties." The stock market crash of 1929 brought that to an abrupt halt and ushered in the Great Depression. The Depression affected not just America, but countries around the world.

With more than one in four people out of work, the U. S. government had to do something. The Smoot-Hawley Tariff Act of 1930 started out as a bill to protect U. S. farmers from having to compete with imported agricultural products. Even as Republican President Herbert Hoover promised voters a "chicken in every pot" during the 1928 presidential campaign, he pledged to provide farmers some relief from falling farm prices due to oversupply in the market.

By the time the legislation came before Congress, however, all sorts of businesses were in serious trouble. The scope of the bill and the size of the tariffs it imposed grew. Lawmakers wanted to close off America's economy from foreign competition. After all, America needed all the jobs it could get. It could not afford to lose any jobs to foreign competition.

The Smoot-Hawley tariff was not much higher than some of America's earlier tariffs had been, notes Ha-Joon Chang at the University of Cambridge. However, other countries were facing a Depression too. They enacted their own higher tariffs.

Imports dropped off dramatically. In 1929, the United States bought $1.3 million in imports from Europe. In 1932, the figure fell to less than $400,000. America's export market shrank too. The United States sold less than $800,000 worth of products to Europe in 1932, down from $2.3 million in 1929.

The protectionist policies failed to boost the economy. Indeed, many economists argue, high tariffs prolonged the Depression. Free trade champions today routinely point to the Smoot-Hawley Act's outcome as proof that protectionism does not pay.

World War II put an end to massive unemployment in America. The war took thousands of men away from home and out of the civilian work force. At the same time, demand increased dramatically in war-related industries.

As World War II neared its end, America and other countries began thinking about the future. If at all possible, they hoped to avoid the economic devastation that followed World War I. A new wave of globalization was about to begin.

A New Beginning at Bretton Woods

Every winter, visitors flock to Bretton Woods in New Hampshire for its world-class skiing and beautiful scenery. During the summer of 1944, however, a meeting at the resort played a pivotal part in economic history. The Allied forces felt the end of the war was near, and they wanted to plan for what would come next. For most of July, 730 delegates from 45 countries met at the resort's Mount Washington Hotel.

One main goal was to rebuild war-ravaged countries and to make financial institutions stable once again. Toward these ends, the attending countries agreed to set up the International Monetary Fund and the International Bank for Reconstruction and Development (now part of the World Bank). These institutions continue to play a part in international economics.

The main goal of the International Monetary Fund (IMF) is to maintain stability in the world economy. Among other things, it deals with issues about exchange rates for different countries' monetary currencies. From the time of the Bretton Woods conference until the 1970s, rates were set relative to the value of gold, which was US $35 per ounce. (Changes in 1971 led to the present system where rates fluctuate, or move up and down.)

The IMF also functions as a "lender of last resort" for governments if their countries cannot cover their payments to other countries. Some controversy exists over the strict terms the IMF imposes on such loans. However, few people question whether an organization such as the IMF should exist.

The World Bank has a slightly different mission, which is primarily to reduce poverty. The World Bank makes loans to countries at little or no interest. It also provides grants and other aid. Within the World Bank, the International Bank for Reconstruction and Development deals mostly with poverty in middle-income countries, while the International Development Association helps the world's poorest countries. By February 2007, 185 countries participated in both the World Bank and the IMF.

The Bretton Woods conference also set the scene for some cooperation on the international economic scene. After the war, countries looked for ways to break down barriers to international trade. They wanted to avoid the widespread protectionism that came after World War I. And they wanted to provide economic stimuli to countries as their economies recovered from the war.

The United Nations had been established in 1945 to promote peace and prevent another world war. Economic leaders wanted a similar regime that could promote free trade among its member countries. As matters stood, countries could not agree on the terms or charter for an International Trade Organization at that time. Nonetheless, they were able to start the world on a path toward freer trade with GATT, the General Agreement on Tariffs and Trade.

Fewer than two dozen countries approved and signed GATT before 1950. Over the years, however, additional countries signed on and took part in the group's eight rounds of multiparty trade negotiations. Many of the concepts and terms agreed to in those rounds of negotiations remain in force under the present World Trade Organization. For now, three points are important.

First, GATT's growing number of parties and scope of trade agreements brought more and more countries into a group whose goal was to reduce tariffs and other trade restrictions. In other words, GATT's express purpose—and that of the WTO today—is to promote free trade.

Second, all trade did not automatically become free trade because of GATT. Each round of negotiations relaxed some restrictions. However, tariffs and other significant trade barriers remain, and their terms are often very complex.

Third, both industrialized and developing countries signed on to GATT. The agreement bound countries only to the extent that they approved different agreements. No single country could dictate the terms of GATT or dominate its negotiations. This became even truer as time progressed and more countries signed on.

Although no country led GATT, a new leader did emerge on the international economic front in the years after World War II—the United States. In contrast to other countries, the United States suffered very few attacks to its own territory. Consequently, it had far less rebuilding to do. The United States was also relatively well off as far as its level of industrialization, available capital, and other economic factors. The economy recovered quickly after the war, and the United States soon became an international economic giant. Promoting free trade was in its interest.

Strong political motives made the United States pursue free trade too. Chief among them was the threat of communism. A communist regime already led the Soviet Union when World War II ended. In 1949, communist forces took over in mainland China too. As the Cold War went on, those countries threatened to convert other governments to communism.

In response, the United States sought to cement its political ties with other countries by promoting capitalism. If countries experienced firsthand the benefits that came from capitalism, America's leaders reasoned, they would feel friendly toward the United States. And they would be less likely to support communist revolutionary movements.

The Marshall Plan, for example, helped rebuild and bolster the economies of Western Europe. European countries also sought to promote freer trade among themselves. Starting in 1952, six countries began the European Coal and Steel Community, which eventually grew into the present-day European Union.

The United States also opened its markets to Japan's growing manufacturing sector. World War II treaties barred Japan from having an army, so that country did not bear substantial defense costs. Soon, it too had a thriving economy.

For the most part, though, this second wave of modern globalization only helped a limited number of industrialized countries. Most of GATT's original member countries were industrialized nations. During the first decades under GATT, the standard of living in the United States, Western Europe, and Japan rose dramatically. From their perspectives, capitalism and international trade were certainly paying off.

By the 1970s, things had changed. The United States and various other countries faced economic recession. Political changes were also under way. After decades of silent opposition, President Richard Nixon opened talks with the government of mainland China during the 1970s. Although tensions still exist between the two countries, those talks paved the path for trade. In 1989, the Soviet Union's communist government collapsed, signaling the end of the

U.S. President Richard Nixon met with Chinese Prime Minister Zhou Enlai in 1972. The historic summit was the first step toward opening up trade between Communist China and the United States.

Cold War. That opened the way for trade with Russia and the Eastern European countries it had dominated since World War II.

New Players and New Developments

Meanwhile, various Asian countries sped up their own industrialization and seized opportunities to attract foreign investment and expand international trade. China, India, and countries in the former Soviet Union all expanded their markets and stepped up international trade. Together, they added approximately 2.5 billion people to the worldmarket in the ten-year period from 1989 to 1999. Singapore, South Korea, Indonesia, and other

Asian countries also stepped up their industrialization and international trade.

With huge populations and widespread poverty, cheap labor became poor countries' big advantage over more industrialized nations. The availability of low-cost labor was not limited to unskilled workers, either. Skilled, technical, and even professional workers commanded far less pay in these countries. Partly, this resulted from those countries' lower standard of living. In many places, workers also lacked bargaining power and other rights that people enjoy in the United States and other industrialized nations. Developing countries also had more relaxed environmental and workplace regulations, tax incentives to attract corporations, and other cost savings.

Companies were very willing to invest in those markets too. Multinational corporations had become commonplace. Moreover, faced with greater competitive pressure, almost all companies welcomed ways to cut costs and increase profits. Outsourcing became more and more common. This is the practice of having certain tasks performed by outside companies rather than in-house. And with modern transportation and telecommunications, companies could do more and more work long-distance. This spurred the growth of offshoring—transferring work abroad to related or independent companies.

By the turn of the twenty-first century, these and other countries were poised to take a leading role in international trade. Indeed, Yale University business professor Jeffrey Garten feels "ten big emerging markets" will play a pivotal role in global economics and politics in the twenty-first century. Garten identifies those markets as China, India, Indonesia, Mexico, Brazil, Argentina, South Africa, Poland, Turkey, and South Korea.

Developments in these countries are already fueling the debate over free trade. Some groups feel their growing role threatens America's workers and its economic well-being. Others argue that free trade fosters disregard for the environment. Still others claim that the most recent beneficiaries of free trade are not in fact playing by the rules and competing on an even playing field. Later chapters will explore these issues. First, it helps to look more closely at economic arguments for liberalizing trade.

3
What a Deal!
Economic Arguments
for Free Trade

Supporters of trade liberalization say it can help all countries achieve net benefits. It promotes competition and efficiency. It gives consumers broader choices and lower prices. And it expands markets for buyers and sellers around the world.

Competition and Competitive Advantage

For most of the time until the nineteenth century, mercantilism directed countries' policies on international trade. Mercantilism holds that a nation's prosperity hinges on its supply of gold and silver.

For mercantilists, the best way to increase a country's wealth is through a positive balance of trade with other countries. A nation's balance of trade is positive when it exports more to other countries than it imports. Other countries' economies must then pay for those exports, either right away or sometime in the future.

Champions of mercantilism presumed that the total volume of global trade was relatively fixed. In other words, they believed the world's wealth was already divided up among various countries. Think of a game where all the play money was already split among the players. The only way to get more for yourself would be to get it from someone else. At the same time, you would want to keep other players from getting their hands on your wealth. Thus, countries had high tariffs and other trade barriers to protect their own producers. Wherever possible, they relied on their own economies. (Conveniently, countries viewed whatever they could extract from colonies as their own, as well.)

Then in 1776, Adam Smith (1723–1790) published *The Wealth of Nations*. Among other things, Smith argued that people prospered more if the forces of competition were allowed to act with less interference from governments. Like an "invisible hand," competition would allocate resources and profits in the way that was most productive and efficient. In Smith's view, countries should import any goods they could not produce as efficiently themselves:

If a foreign country can supply us with a commodity cheaper than we ourselves can make it, better buy it of them with some part of the produce of our own industry, employed in a way in which we have some advantage.

When governments tried to protect domestic industries from imports, they removed competitive pressure. In Smith's view, that led to inefficiency—domestic companies did not have to try as hard to make high-quality, low-cost products. That reduced overall wealth.

Later economists moved further away from mercantil-

BRITISH ECONOMIST DAVID RICARDO PROMOTED THE CONCEPT OF COMPARATIVE ADVANTAGE AS A JUSTIFICATION FOR FREE TRADE BETWEEN COUNTRIES.

ism. In England, David Ricardo (1772–1823) advanced the concept of comparative advantage in his book, *Principles of Political Economy and Taxation*. Writings by other English economists, including James Mill (1773–1836) and Robert Torrens (1814–1884), support the concept, but Ricardo is most famous for the idea.

The theory of comparative advantage says the central issue is not whether one country can make something more efficiently than another. Rather, the question is where each country's greatest strength lies, compared to the other. Under the theory of comparative advantage, a country should devote its resources to producing at home whatever it does most efficiently. It should then import other items.

At first blush, it seems strange to say a country should buy something from another country that does not have an absolute advantage in making that product. But what matters is not just how efficiently a country makes one product. A big issue is also what profits a country would give up by not making another product. Economists refer to that lost income as opportunity cost.

As a simple example, suppose you can make $10 per hour making screwdrivers, but only $6 per hour making wrenches. If that were true, you would want to concentrate on making screwdrivers. Otherwise, for each hour you spent making wrenches, you would be giving up $4 you could have earned making screwdrivers.

In international trade, countries want to maximize their incomes too. When opportunity cost is taken into account, a country does best by concentrating on whatever it can make most efficiently relative to what other countries produce. Note this is different from having an absolute advantage over the other countries. Even if one country can make multiple products more efficiently than other countries, it should still focus on the area where it is relatively better. Even after importing the other products from places, the country comes out ahead.

To illustrate, Ricardo provided an example involving England and Portugal and two products—wool cloth and wine. Even if Portugal could make both items more cheaply, Ricardo said it should concentrate on the area where it had the bigger advantage relative to England. In his example, this was wine.

With international trade, Portugal could sell some of its wine to England. And it could use some income to import English wool cloth. Likewise, England would be better off focusing on the product where it had a comparative advantage, which was wool cloth in Ricardo's example. Both countries would wind up with more income with international trade than without it. Thus, trade would be a win-win situation for both countries.

Mehrene Larudee at DePaul University suggests another way of looking at comparative advantage. Again, consider a simple example where Portugal made both wine and wool cloth more efficiently than England, and those are the only two products made by both countries. England would want to buy some of those cheaper products. However, it would need money to do that, so it would have to sell something to Portugal. To do that, England would keep offering one of its goods more cheaply, such as cloth, until it had a comparative advantage over Portugal in that area. Then the issue of opportunity costs would make Portugal want to buy English cloth. And England would be better off with trade because it would get cheaper wine.

Baseball can help explain the theory of comparative advantage too, says economics professor Edward Scahill at the University of Scranton. Just look at Babe Ruth. Born George Herman Ruth Jr. (1895–1948), "the Babe" started his professional baseball career as a pitcher for the Boston Red Sox. From 1915 to 1919, Ruth excelled among his teammates in both pitching and hitting, leading the Red Sox to the World Series in 1918. During 1918 and 1919, he split his playing time for the Red Sox between the outfield and the pitching staff. Then the Red Sox traded Ruth to the Yankees in 1920, and Boston did not win the World Series again until 2004.

Yankees manager Miller Huggins decided to play Ruth exclusively as an outfielder and hitter, rather than a pitcher. While Ruth was good at both, he was better as a hitter compared to the rest of the team. And while he was better than most pitchers, he was not as superior to them. Other team members can play almost every game, while pitchers must rest several days between games. Having Ruth play as a hitter maximized the chances for the team to benefit from his hitting skills. It also gave fans more opportunities to see him in action, which boosted attendance at games.

Huggins's strategy paid off. In 1920, the Yankees finished in third place, and the following year, the team won its first American League championship. By putting Ruth where he had the greatest comparative advantage, Scahill argues, the Yankees made the best use of his strengths and maximized their profits.

As great as the benefits of comparative advantage might be, they are eaten away or erased when countries impose tariffs and other trade barriers. True, keeping imports out could protect domestic industries temporarily. And the country blocked from the market would lose some profits. But both countries lose out on some gains they would have enjoyed without the trade barriers. Ricardo thus viewed tariffs as especially pernicious, or harmful:

The sole effect of high duties on the importation either of manufactures or of corn, or of a bounty on their exportation, is to divert a portion of capital to an employment, which it would not naturally

seek. It causes a pernicious distribution of the general funds of the society - it bribes a manufacturer to commence or continue in a comparatively less profitable employment. It is the worst species of taxation, for it does not give to the foreign country all that it takes away from the home country, the balance of loss being made up by the less advantageous distribution of the general capital.

To understand why this would happen, think about how supply and demand affect price. In economics, supply relates to the quantity of a product available in the market. Demand deals with how many buyers in the market want that product.

High demand for a product in short supply generally makes the price rise. Buyers who are willing and able to pay the higher price get the product. Others lose out.

At the same time, other people see the high profits to be made in that industry. Thus, more people begin making the product, and supply increases. Now producers want to make sure they can sell all their supply, so they drop the price. As the supply increases, however, people no longer need to outbid each other, and the price drops. However, if the price drops too much, making the product may no longer be as profitable as other businesses might be. If and when that happens, some of the suppliers would switch to other industries.

Eventually, the market would come into balance, or equilibrium. The point at which supply and demand are equal would thus determine the price for the product. The same process would take place simultaneously for all the other products sold in the market. As supply and demand fluctuate for different items, the "invisible hand" of free market competition should guide all factors of production to their best and highest use. That, in turn, would maximize prosperity for the economy as a whole.

Barriers to free trade interfere with what would otherwise happen in a competitive marketplace. In other words, they affect prices, making certain industries seem more or less profitable and efficient than they actually are. To avoid this and be sure everyone reaps the maximum benefits from trade, supporters say the world needs as few barriers to trade as possible.

Under Ricardo's theory, all countries get the most net benefits when everyone removes barriers to trade. However, countries do not have to wait until everyone else acts. They can still realize some economic benefits by lowering their own barriers to trade.

The last point is often counterintuitive, because many people see trade concessions as giving up something. Or, they may focus on the advantage gained by sellers of imported goods. Yet while those sellers gain a foothold in the market, consumers get lower prices as a result of competition. Stiffer competition encourages efficiency in domestic industries too. For staunch free trade champions, keeping trade barriers just because other countries have them is counterproductive.

Many, if not most, mainstream economists still support the theory of comparative advantage. Some disagree, however, on whether the theory really explains what happens in today's marketplace, and whether it justifies all the policy changes that supporters of trade liberalization seek.

Theory vs. Real Life

Today's world, of course, has far more countries and many more products than the two Ricardo talked about in his example of English wool cloth and Portuguese wine. And competition comes from everywhere. Deciding where one's comparative advantage lies can be very complex.

The real world is constantly changing too. And with today's rate of technological change, it is harder than ever

Supply and Demand

As a group, economists love mathematics and graphs. For a product where supply and demand could both vary in response to price, an economist might use an illustration like this. On the graph, the vertical axis stands for price, while the horizontal axis represents quantity. Both values increase as they move away from zero. The supply curve represents the amount of the product that the sellers are willing to produce at different prices. The demand curve represents the number of people willing and able to buy a product at different prices.

When a product's price is very high, relatively few buyers are willing and able to pay that price. Conversely, when supply is much lower than demand, the price will be very high. The quantity of the product sold at that high price will thus be rather low.

On the other hand, suppose that supply of a product exceeds the demand for it. The price will drop to a lower point as sellers try to attract more buyers.

The price at equilibrium in a free and competitive market would be the point where supply equals demand:

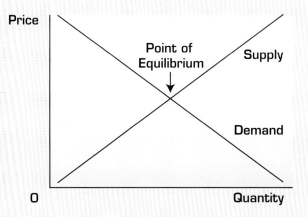

Tariffs or other trade barriers would discourage people from buying imports, since their cost would be artificially high. That would lead to inefficiency, and the market would not reach the lower equilibrium point price that buyers might otherwise have had.

to keep up. One country may have a comparative advantage in producing screwdrivers now, but that advantage could shift to another country in the future. The change could take years, or it could happen in just a few months. Over time, economies adjust to changes. In the meantime, people going through those adjustments can suffer significant losses.

Also, some factors of production may not transfer easily to other fields. This especially becomes a problem in industries that require large initial investments of capital, or significant expenses for training and education. Making a move becomes especially risky if any comparative advantage might quickly disappear once other countries catch up.

Today's capital markets make it possible to invest around the world. Many businesses are not limited to a single country, either. Thousands of multinational companies do business around the globe, with General Electric, Exxon Mobil, and Shell ranking among the largest.

Economist and journalist Philippe Legrain notes that some multinational companies' outputs even exceed the GDP of entire nations. Other economists argue this is like comparing apples and oranges. In any case, some multinational companies have huge volumes of business. Their actions thus influence what happens in the world of international trade.

Technology has also expanded the universe of what countries can trade. Ricardo's theory of comparative advantage focused on trade in goods. Thanks to modern transportation and telecommunications, countries now trade billions of dollars worth of services each year too. In some cases, that has caused shifts in countries' comparative advantages.

In today's world, Ricardo's theory of comparative advantage still sometimes leaves everyone better off. But that

OUTSOURCING LETS COMPANIES OFFER TECHNICAL SUPPORT SERVICES AROUND-THE-CLOCK. FREE TRADE SUPPORTERS SAY THAT OUTSOURCING PROVIDES IMPROVED SERVICE AT BETTER PRICES. FREE TRADE CRITICS COMPLAIN THAT IT DEPRIVES U.S. WORKERS OF GOOD JOBS.

is not always the case, cautions Paul Samuelson at the Massachusetts Institute of Technology. To show that workers' real wages can sometimes go down as a result of trade, he uses a hypothetical situation where China gets a comparative advantage in an area where the United States had previously had an advantage. The changes in wages then depend on whether and how the shift in comparative advantage draws jobs from another country. Outsourcing, for example, can sometimes cause jobs to leave permanently. If that happens, the country losing some of its comparative advantage can end up with lower real wages from "dynamic fair free trade."

Acting Alone?

While mutual reductions in trade barriers are helpful, countries still get economic benefits by reducing tariffs and other restrictions unilaterally, or on their own. The World Bank estimates that roughly two-thirds of the reductions in tariffs that took place between 1983 and 2003 resulted from moves that were, for the most part, unilateral. Argentina, Brazil, China, and India, for example, all undertook reforms aimed at increasing their domestic economies' productivity.

Nonetheless, countries still maintain barriers to trade. Sometimes the reasons are political. Despite the theoretical gains, people in many countries see reductions in trade barriers as giving up something.

Dropping trade barriers may involve other costs too. Think about a student who wants his parents to do his homework for him. If they did, the student would not learn the material. Developing nations face "exactly that kind of a trade-off," says Mark Weisbrot at the Center for Economic and Policy Research:

> You can get the gains from trade by getting the most advanced, cheap imports immediately. Or, you can develop a process to produce them yourself and then become a developed country.
>
> Of course, you want to have some of both, right? You want to be able to import the things that will actually help your development, and keep out the stuff that keeps you from developing your own industries where you think as a country you can do better. . . .
>
> [A]lmost no country has really gotten to the rich club of nations by just opening their borders

to everything. And it probably won't ever happen that way.

During our country's early days, Alexander Hamilton urged a protectionist policy for the United States' infant industries. High tariffs helped America build its own economy. Other industrialized nations had similar policies. Developing nations can argue that they, too, should have the chance to let their own industries grow. Otherwise, even if they are no longer technically colonies, they would remain dependent on industrialized countries.

Former Senator Ernest Hollings (D–SC) says history also justifies renewed barriers to trade in the United States. America's economy "was built on managed trade or protectionism." However, he argues, U.S. trade policies in the last twenty years have harmed the country's economy. In Hollings's view, America needs protectionism again, for "rebuilding the country."

Can It Keep Up?

The United States now imports far more in goods and services than it exports. In 2005, the United States as a whole bought nearly $724 billion more in goods and services than it sold to other countries.

All signs are that international trade will continue to increase. Movements that promote free trade will likely speed that increase. Can the United States continue with current trading patterns on a long-term basis? Experts disagree.

Individuals who run up huge debts run into trouble when creditors demand to be paid. If they cannot consistently make payments, they wind up in bankruptcy. Common sense suggests that the same would hold true for the country's economy as a whole.

Even Ricardo recognized that trade cannot be a one-way deal. "No country can long import unless it also exports, or can long export unless it also imports," he wrote. Indeed, richer countries will suffer "more distress" from fast changes in trade patterns, because they have a lot of capital tied up in machinery and other fixed assets.

If America cannot make timely payments on all that it imports, its economy could be in serious trouble. The worst-case scenario would be if all creditor countries wanted full payment at once. A serious financial crisis could result.

On the other hand, the United States is a leader in global trade, and its government has been stable. Other countries may not worry as much as they might if debts mounted up for a smaller and poorer nation. Moreover, foreign investors already have substantial assets in the United States. Causing an economic crisis is not in their self-interest.

Free trade critics find little comfort in this. At some point, Americans must still pay for whatever they import. They also worry whether America can really stay "independent" as it relies more and more on foreign businesses and their products.

Arguing With Numbers

An old joke tells about an economist, an engineer, and a physicist on a desert island with a single can of beans. The engineer and physicist strategize about ways to crack the can open or explode it with heat. But the economist just says, "Assume we have a can opener."

In real life, the wrong assumptions can lead to wrong or useless conclusions. Economists differ about what assumptions they make, and in how they measure economic factors. Thus, reputable economists often disagree with each other.

U.S. Balance of Trade in Goods

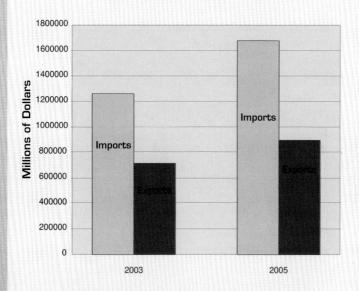

Although America's exports of goods grew between 2003 and 2005, its imports grew even more.

Source: Organization for Economic Co-Operation and Development, "Dataset: Balance of Payments, United States," data extracted October 16, 2006. http://stats.oecd.org/wbos/default.aspx?datasetcode=MEI_BOP (accessed October 16, 2006).

Also, while overall economic effects of trade may sound huge, the extent of percentage changes may be more meaningful. Suppose trade increases a country's GDP by $1 billion. If its population is 200 million people, per capita income goes up only $5. If average income was $600 to start with, it would then be $605. The country would still welcome the extra billion dollars. However, the average person's lifestyle would not improve much—even if the benefits actually flowed to everyone instead of staying with the wealthiest group in society.

4
Deal Us In!
The WTO and Other
Trading Alliances

As the uproar in Hong Kong, Seattle, and elsewhere showed, gatherings of the World Trade Organization spark controversy and protests. Nonetheless, the WTO's stated goal is to promote freer trade, and its members include both rich and poor countries. WTO members all hope to expand their markets and boost their economic well-being through trade.

This chapter explores how the WTO works, along with criticisms of that organization. It also looks at how regional and other trading groups fit into the overall scheme of foreign trade.

What Is the WTO?

The WTO builds upon and expands the agreements that existed under GATT, the General Agreement on Tariffs and Trade. Its membership is also larger. Twenty-three countries signed on to the first GATT agreement, which became effective in 1948. By the time the WTO began its official life in 1995, GATT had grown to 128 signatory countries. By January 2007, the WTO had 150 members, with several more countries applying to join.

Today the WTO provides a basic framework for countries to meet, negotiate, and hopefully agree upon terms for international trade. General terms and principles for conducting trade are set out in the WTO's General Agreement on Tariffs and Trade (the WTO's GATT), the General Agreement on Trade in Services (GATS), and the agreement on Trade-Related Aspects of Intellectual Property Rights (TRIPS). Other agreements address particular issues, such as standards, technical barriers to trade, and investment. Beyond these agreements, the WTO provides a forum for countries to settle trade disputes.

WTO agreements are essentially treaties that must be approved by member governments. Thus, WTO members can only be countries (and some territories). Individuals or nongovernmental organizations (NGOs) cannot join.

The WTO does its day-to-day work in Geneva, Switzerland, with a staff of about 635 people. The Director-General heads the organization; in 2007, that individual was Pascal Lamy of France. Individual countries may have ministers and representatives in Geneva. Countries also participate in different conferences and coalitions among the WTO's members.

The WTO's Ministerial Conference includes representatives of all the member governments. It meets at least every two years, although negotiations continue among representatives in between.

Major agreements often take years to negotiate and finalize. One reason is the complexity and sensitivity of different subjects. Nations want other countries to open their markets. Yet they are often wary about how opening their own markets will affect people at home. Beyond this, representatives need time to obtain their own countries' approval or rejection of different proposals. Often, this process involves several stages. Thus, it is common to talk about "rounds" of negotiations in the WTO.

Generally, a round takes its name from where the new set of negotiations started. Creation of the WTO resulted from the Uruguay round of negotiations under GATT, which lasted from 1986 to 1994. As of 2006, the WTO was still working on issues from the Doha Development Agenda. That round of negotiations began in Doha, Qatar, in 2001.

In principle, all countries are equal in the WTO. Every member country can decide whether to agree to proposed trade terms. Arguably, then, every member country has a similar "vote" or "veto" on whether the organization achieves a consensus.

The consensus approach has several benefits. In theory, it avoids the problem of having a majority of member nations "gang up" and impose their will on other countries. It preserves the sovereignty of member nations, because the organization does not formally make any country accept particular trade terms. (Sovereignty is a country's right to rule or control its own actions.) The consensus approach also acknowledges that every member nation is important, since all must consent in order to make agreements binding.

In practice, however, little progress can occur unless the organization's biggest trading members want to enter into an agreement. The WTO itself recognizes that major agreements often require an initial breakthrough from the WTO's "Quad": The United States, the European Union (as a group), Canada, and Japan.

The WTO would be too unwieldy if every member country took part in all stages of negotiations, explains political science professor Fiona McGillivray at New York University. Instead, representatives of the major supplier and buyer countries try to reach a mutually acceptable position. As of 2000, about 40 percent of all world trade involved the United States and European Union. Thus, they usually appear on one side or the other of major WTO negotiations.

While this seems efficient, the process often excludes developing countries from important stages of negotiations. Supporters of the WTO do not worry about this. Negotiated terms still require agreement from other nations before they become binding. Also, WTO agreements sometimes allow more lenient terms to poorer nations.

Nevertheless, groups like Greenpeace and Public Citizen complain that the WTO lets richer trading countries exert significant pressure on smaller nations, especially poor ones. Indeed, because agreements will not come about unless the larger, industrialized countries agree, critics claim that the process lets those nations exploit other countries. Industrialized nations rarely agree to terms that hurt their own interests, like fewer farm subsidies or less protection for intellectual property. Yet, critics say, they want developing countries to drop other types of trade barriers.

WTO critics also complain that too much of the organization's activities take place behind closed doors, without transcripts and formal voting. Similar complaints focus on how the WTO hears and decides trade disputes. McGillivray generally sides with the WTO on the issue of transcripts and records. Representative governments generally do not make all materials available to the public. More importantly, the WTO is not a government. Rather, it is "a set of rules" for negotiating international agreements and dealing with disputes.

However, even President Bill Clinton, who supported free trade agreements, complained about the WTO's "secret proceedings" after the 1999 protests in Seattle:

[T]hey're going to have to open the process so that the voices of labor, the environment and the developing countries can be heard; and so that the decisions are transparent, the records are open, and the consequences are clear.

Unless proceedings and records are open, critics say, people cannot trust the WTO.

In 2006, the WTO announced that all official GATT documents from before 1995 would be made public. "Providing access to these historic documents is a further sign of the WTO's commitment to transparency," said Lamy. The decision will help scholars and historians. However, it will not resolve critics' complaints about current decision-making.

Governing Principles

Rules in the WTO's agreements incorporate some ideas from the initial GATT in 1947, plus others developed over the years. In general, WTO members agree to trade between and among each other without discrimination. If a country gives favorable trading terms to one nation, it should give the same favorable terms to all other WTO members. This is called most-favored nation treatment, or nondiscrimination. Basically, it is as if WTO member countries agree with each other, "Look, we'll all give each other the best deal available." Some exceptions apply, especially for free trade groups, as discussed later.

National treatment is another basic principle. Each WTO member agrees to treat products and services from foreign suppliers the same as those from domestic sources.

Ideally, the principle of national treatment will let identical items compete with each other on an equal basis, regardless of where they come from. The WTO agreements say imports and domestic products should get equal treatment.

The WTO agreements still let countries use standards to protect the public from potentially unsafe imports. However, the rules must be the same ones that they use for their own products. Any standards that affect imports must also be "science-based," instead of resting on speculation.

Controversy also arises when countries keep imports out based on standards that may not affect the final product. Potential importers may cry foul. But labor advocates care deeply if a product is produced with child labor or in unsafe working conditions. Other groups worry when imports are produced in ways that, in their view, threaten the environment.

Before imports can compete on the same basis as domestic products, they have to get into a country. For example, it should not matter whether a baseball bat is made in the United States or Japan. During the 1980s and early 1990s, however, Japanese rules and delays in customs inspections made it very hard for American manufacturers to sell aluminum bats in Japan. The WTO calls on members to cut such "red tape" and other nontariff barriers.

The WTO discourages import limits, export targets, or other types of quotas. Likewise, a law that called for a certain percentage of a product to come from domestic raw materials would generally go against WTO agreements. Although it might help local industry and economic development, it would block imports that did not meet the local-content requirement.

Intellectual property is the subject of the WTO's TRIPS agreement. It calls upon members to respect and enforce each other's copyrights, trademarks, and patents. The TRIPS agreement's goal is to reassure countries that they can safely engage in international trade in technology, entertainment, medicine, and other areas.

Intellectual property laws grant copyrights, trademarks, and patents as a way to encourage innovation. The laws shield qualifying inventors, authors, artists, and companies from competition for a limited period of time. Such protection makes sure they receive their share of the profits from their ideas.

About half of the United States' exports depend on intellectual property rights in technology, entertainment, drugs, and other areas. It probably stands to lose most if other nations have lax enforcement. People who want to protect American industries complain that the WTO does not effectively enforce the TRIPS agreement. In their view, that is like looking the other way while someone steals.

Other critics say TRIPS shows that the WTO really helps rich countries and big corporations. They argue that TRIPS really restricts trade, by cutting down on international competition.

In any case, the WTO says its general goal is to promote free trade. However, free trade does not happen all at once. Rather, the WTO deals with issues in different negotiating rounds. Countries typically phase in changes, or make them in steps. Developing countries often have even more time to meet any new requirements.

Gradual change gives countries' economies time to adjust. One criticism, however, is that the order in which the WTO addresses issues can give priority to interests of richer countries and postpone progress on things that matter most to poorer nations.

The WTO also wants predictability. When member nations feel confident that trade barriers will not rise in the future, they are more comfortable making investments and pursuing trade. Agreements that bind members to particular terms have the practical effect of locking them in for the future. If the country wants to raise trade barriers later, it must negotiate with the other nations, or provide some compensation for lost trade.

In one sense, most treaties lock in nations to their terms. On the other hand, critics feel the WTO's emphasis on binding terms takes away some of the flexibility countries would otherwise have over how they trade with others. Binding terms also affect countries' ability to change domestic laws that could arguably be seen as trade barriers. They could enact such domestic laws anyway, but then they could face retaliatory action under the WTO agreements.

Meanwhile, economist Andrew Rose at the University of California, Berkeley, claims there is no evidence that WTO membership actually makes trade more stable and predictable. It is also unclear whether any benefits outweigh nations' loss of flexibility.

Although the WTO rules are broad, they have important exceptions. In various cases, more lenient conditions apply to developing nations. The rationale is that they need flexibility for their economies to adjust to trade liberalization, as well as help for newer industries to grow. As discussed later, the extent to which WTO trade rules actually help poor countries is very much in debate.

Oversight and Dispute Resolution

To make sure that members comply with agreements, the WTO requires countries to inform the organization of various policy changes and actions on trade. Beyond this, the WTO's Trade Policy Review Body regularly reviews countries' trade programs. The Trade Policy Review Body has essentially the same membership as the WTO's General Council.

The WTO also lets nations protect themselves from unfair actions by other countries. Article 6 of the WTO's GATT sets out detailed procedures for countries to protect their own industries from harm when foreign nations export products at artificially low prices. Similarly, WTO agreements prohibit certain subsidies and let nations take actions to counter their effects. Countries can also take steps to protect against a sudden surge in imports.

At a minimum, countries taking such actions must notify the WTO. More detailed and complex rules apply in each case as well. Because of the amounts of money involved, such matters often cause considerable controversy.

As and when other disputes arise, countries can use the WTO's dispute resolution process. Basically, it is an arbitration process. One or more countries file a complaint against one or more other WTO members. The complaining and defending nations must see if they can settle the dispute. If not, a panel of neutral experts from three or five countries considers evidence and arguments. Often the panel issues a preliminary report, which the parties can comment on. The panel then makes a final decision on who is right and who is wrong.

If a party disagrees with the panel's decision, it can appeal to the WTO's Dispute Settlement Body. Three members of a seven-member Appellate Body then hear the case. As a group, the three decide whether to accept or reject the panel's recommendation.

At all steps in the proceeding, the WTO panels' primary concern is application and interpretation of the WTO agreements, versus separate treaties or other concerns. As shown by the environmental cases discussed later, critics consider the approach to be too focused on commercial interests and too much of a limit on governments' sovereignty.

Unlike courts that can call on police to enforce their orders, the WTO cannot force countries to obey its decisions on disputes. Losing members often obey in response to the pressures of international public opinion. If a country does not comply, however, the WTO lets the winning countries retaliate. For example, they can raise tariffs and other barriers to keep the other country's products out. Ideally, the financial incentive in continued exports can help persuade countries to comply with WTO rulings.

As a practical matter, a small country may account for such a tiny part of a large country's trade that its retaliation would have little impact. Meanwhile, a small country could hurt itself by erecting barriers to imports its economy needs. It would be like a gnat trying to ram into an elephant—much more painful for the gnat than the elephant. Even where countries are on relatively equal terms as trading partners, retaliation can deprive both countries of the benefits from international trade. Thus, while a country can retaliate if the losing party will not abide by the WTO's decision, it is not a complete "win."

Separate Deals

Apart from the WTO, countries enter into other bilateral (two-party) and multilateral (more than two parties) trading arrangements. The WTO expressly recognizes that countries may make such agreements and allows an exception to the general principle of nondiscrimination. Under Article 24 of the WTO's GATT, countries may enter into regional trading arrangements that cover "substantially all" trade within the group. Also, nonparticipating countries should not face any higher barriers to trade after the agreement than before. The WTO calls on countries to register such pacts, so it can review them and make sure they comply with Article 24. In practice, however, the WTO rarely rules on submissions.

Why do countries bother with bilateral and multilateral arrangements when they have the WTO? For one thing, such groups make it possible for parties to lower or completely drop certain trade barriers on a mutual basis where they might not otherwise be able to get the rest of the WTO to agree. In that sense, the terms of trade in bilateral and multilateral trading arrangements differ from across-the-board tariffs, quotas, or other restrictions that would apply to any country's imports. Such agreements also let countries pursue mutual interests in regional development or other areas.

Political considerations also come into play, as government leaders consider potential effects of trade policies on different industries. Even if the policy changes produce net benefits, some groups will see the reductions as a concession, where the country gives something up. Politicians can sell trade policies to voters more easily when other countries are willing to make mutual changes.

Beyond this, unilateral reductions give up some of a country's "bargaining chips" for getting concessions from other countries. After all, mutual reductions in trade barriers are a better deal than unilateral moves. The mutual reductions open markets in other countries and make it easier to export goods there.

As of 2005, the World Bank reported there were over 225 regional trading agreements, with another five dozen in the process of negotiation. Almost every country was a party to at least one agreement. Many were in multiple arrangements, for an average of six in general and thirteen for northern, industrialized countries.

Listing and describing all the agreements would be impractical here. Nonetheless, a few of the larger and better-known trading groups show some of the types of arrangements countries make.

NAFTA, the North American Free Trade Agreement, caused significant national debate when the United States negotiated this pact with Canada and Mexico in the early 1990s. Since January 1, 1994, NAFTA has dropped tariffs and various other barriers to trade among the three countries. Side agreements contained detailed provisions meant to deal with concerns about the environment and labor.

Free trade supporters say the pact has helped all three countries. As support, they point to the fact that Mexico and Canada are the United States' largest trading partners. With the countries sharing the goal of regional development and growth, supporters say it only makes sense to have free trade among them.

However, NAFTA remains controversial. Critics say the pact benefits investors far more than consumers and workers. Among other things, the AFL-CIO and the Economic Policy Institute claim that NAFTA has cost the United States over one million jobs.

CAFTA, the Central American Free Trade Agreement, will deal with trade among the United States, the Dominican Republic, El Salvador, Guatemala, Honduras, Nicaragua, and Costa Rica. Congress approved the agreement, modeled upon NAFTA, in 2005. CAFTA has also received significant opposition from free trade critics, both in the United States and abroad. By 2006, all the countries had ratified the treaty except Costa Rica, where approval was still pending.

The European Union (EU) promotes the free movement of people, goods, services, and money among the nations that make up its membership. Twenty-five states were full members as of 2006, with five more in the process of joining or seeking membership.

The EU has existed in its present form since 1992. However its beginnings date back to 1951, when France, Italy, West Germany, Belgium, Luxembourg, and the Netherlands founded the European Coal and Steel Community. Starting in 1958, the group became the European Economic Community (also called the Common Market). It eventually expanded to become a full customs union for virtually all goods. Basically, this means that

Who Negotiates for the U.S.?

Working out the details of international trade agreements falls to the Office of the United States Trade Representative (USTR). This agency within the federal government's executive branch has over two hundred people. The United States Trade Representative heads the agency and is part of the Cabinet. The president nominates him or her, subject to confirmation by the Senate. As of late 2006, the United States Trade Representative was Susan Schwab.

In general, the USTR supports and promotes the president's political policies. It gathers input and feedback from legislators, business organizations, and public interest groups. It also consults with other executive agencies. Using all information at hand, the agency tries to negotiate the best deals it can in the WTO and through other trading agreements.

The president has final authority to accept any deal negotiated by the USTR. Before any agreement can be binding, it requires approval from Congress as well. Congress also must pass any laws needed to implement the trade agreement.

From time to time, Congress has agreed to allow "fast-track" or "trade authorities procedures" approval of trade agreements. This means that Congress can debate the pros and cons of the deal, but cannot change it. After debate, the agreement is subject to a yes or no vote. Critics say such processes short-cut the legislative functions of debate and amendments. Supporters say streamlined approval makes it easier for the United States to negotiate in the international arena.

THE TEAMSTERS UNION AND VARIOUS OTHER GROUPS PROTEST THAT NAFTA AND OTHER FREE TRADE AGREEMENTS HAVE BEEN BAD DEALS FOR AMERICAN AND MEXICAN WORKERS.

trade between members had practically no barriers. The effect was to let buyers and sellers in member states trade with each other similar to the way interstate trade takes place in the United States.

Today, the EU has more than four times the original number of Common Market members. It also has substantially broader powers. EU countries are still independent, sovereign nations. However, the EU also deals with environmental, health, money, energy, and other issues through the European Parliament, the European Commission, and the Court of Justice. Member countries use the euro as a common currency. They also share foreign and security policy.

The EU had roughly 460 million people within its

twenty-five member countries as of 2005. A majority are industrialized democracies that are comparatively wealthy. The remainder includes some countries that adopted democratic governments since the fall of communist governments in the 1980s. Due to its size, wealth, and volume of trade, the EU is a formidable alliance that has significant bargaining power in the international arena.

About two-thirds of the member countries' imports and exports came from and went to other EU countries in 2004. As for non-EU trading partners, the United States had the largest volume of both imports and exports. However, the value of imports from the United States dropped by roughly 40 million euros from 2001 to 2004. Meanwhile, EU imports from China doubled in the five years since 1999, to more than 125 million euros in 2004.

Over 200 additional trade arrangements exist between and among countries outside the WTO structure. Mercosur serves as the South American Common Market. African groups include the East African Community, the West African Economic and Monetary Union, and the Southern African Customs Union. Asian trade groups include the Association of Southeast Asian Nations. Australia and New Zealand cooperate through the Australia-New Zealand Closer Economic Relations Trade Agreement. The dozens of other trade pacts include treaties such as the free trade agreements between the United States and Chile, and the United States and Israel.

The WTO still plays a leading role in the free trade movement and the accompanying debate over free trade. Nonetheless, the large number of separate agreements shows that the WTO is not the sole organization involved. Moreover, many governments from both large and small countries have decided that it is in their interests to join one or more such groups. As different agreements come up for approval, both supporters and detractors of the free trade movement will voice their opinions.

5
A Rotten Deal for Workers

The year 2006 began with bad news for American autoworkers. General Motors had already announced it would cut 30,000 jobs in late 2005. Then Ford Motor Company said it would slash up to 30,000 jobs and close at least a dozen plants by 2012. Meanwhile, Daimler-Chrysler reported plans for 6,000 layoffs.

America's former "big three" automakers all faced disappointing North American sales. At the same time, huge health-care costs for employees, pension obligations, and other duties under union contracts imposed high costs. But foreign competition also played a big part in the cuts. Indeed, the auto industry had already had huge job losses. From 2000 to 2006, the United States' auto industry cut about 15 percent of its workforce, and 200,000 jobs vanished.

Critics say free trade and globalization are draining America of its jobs. At the same time, they say, companies exploit workers abroad. How can this happen, and how do supporters of trade liberalization respond?

Where Have All the Jobs Gone?

As the automobile industry shows, international trade places competitive pressure on domestic companies, especially when foreign products cost less. Price differences exist because market conditions in other countries often let employers pay their workers significantly less. Foreign workers may also lack the bargaining power and rights that many Americans have through their unions. Foreign laws may provide fewer workplace protections as well.

Foreign commerce is not limited to what people think

MEMBERS OF BANGLADESH WORKING WOMEN ATTEND A PROTEST MARCH DEMANDING BETTER LABOR CONDITIONS. CRITICS OF FREE TRADE SAY IT PROMOTES EXPLOITATION OF WORKERS, ESPECIALLY WOMEN AND CHILDREN.

of as finished goods, either. Even when a car is "built" in the United States, the brakes, electronics, and other parts may come from Singapore, China, Mexico, and other countries. Partial assembly work often happens abroad as well. Ironically, a Toyota, Honda, Nissan, or other "foreign" brand auto sometimes has more work done on it in the United States than the traditional "American" brands.

Sometimes companies buy parts from foreign producers. Other times, multinational companies import products and parts from their own foreign subsidiaries or divisions. One United Nations estimate put the number of multinational companies at over 60,000 worldwide, although a much smaller number account for most production and trade. As this century began, America's General Electric and ExxonMobil held the top two spots, as ranked by foreign assets.

Along with this phenomenon, industries are shifting elsewhere. Automobile parts manufacturing has gone from places like Wisconsin and New Jersey to Mexico and Thailand. Making heating and air conditioning units has gone from Syracuse, New York, to Singapore and Malaysia. The refrigerator industry left Illinois for Mexico. Meanwhile, computer parts manufacturing has moved to China and other Asian countries.

America's textile industry has suffered too. Since the 1920s, its mills and factories have competed with manufacturers in Japan, China, Mexico, Latin America, and other countries. Within the last twenty years, the competition has become even fiercer.

Consider the case of Kannapolis, North Carolina. At their peak, the town's textile mills employed roughly 20,000 people. Starting in the 1980s, automation cut many of those jobs. By the late 1990s, the local Cannon plant employed just 4,300 workers. Nevertheless, at age thirty-five, Robert Brawley made $17 per hour on the night shift.

Then on July 31, 2003, Pillowtex Corporation, which owned the Cannon brand, filed for bankruptcy. The company felt it could no longer compete against cheaper imports from India, Pakistan, China, and Brazil. Suddenly, over four thousand people in Kannapolis and elsewhere had no jobs and no health insurance. When Robert Brawley finally found employment with a box manufacturer eleven months later, his new job paid only half of his prior wages. Another textile worker, Leann Harrington, felt lucky to work at a café for just $3 per hour plus tips.

A few thousand jobs here, a couple of hundred there, and several dozen elsewhere all add up. Conservative commentator Patrick Buchanan estimates that at least 2.6 million manufacturing jobs have left the United States since 1980. Like Robert Brawley and Leann Harrington, many displaced workers eventually find other jobs. But those jobs often pay far less.

Independent candidate and businessman Ross Perot lost the 1992 presidential election to Bill Clinton. But he scored big points with many Americans when he argued against NAFTA in 1993. "NAFTA will cause a giant sucking sound as jobs go south," Perot warned, playing on fears that American companies would shift jobs to Mexico.

Fear of the "giant sucking sound" of jobs leaving for Mexico or other low-wage countries still strikes a chord with many workers. Unskilled laborers have been hit hardest, but jobs requiring higher education have gone too.

"Just as with the move of manufacturing overseas, you're going to see an increasing flux of technical jobs out of the U.S.," noted Craig Barrett of Intel. "We don't have any protected domains anymore." California's "Silicon Valley" was once the center of computer and information technology (IT) worldwide. By 2004, however, Bangalore, India, had 150,000 IT engineers—approximately 20,000 more than Silicon Valley.

With modern travel and telecommunications, workers can do many tasks overseas, either through subsidiaries and divisions, or through outsourcing to independent companies. Outsourcing also helps companies offer phone support around the clock. For example, workers on the Indian day shift can help customers who call from America during the night. The night shift deals with many customers who call during daylight hours in their own countries. Call centers are also big business in South Africa, Egypt, Latin America, and the Philippines.

Free trade critics say Americans should be very afraid. By 2009, a Deloitte Research study predicts, the financial sector will outsource two million jobs to foreign markets. Jobs in business management, architecture, the life sciences, and even law are likely to be lost to overseas competition too. In all, a Forrester Research study reported, America could lose over 3.3 million white-collar jobs by 2015. Critics like Lou Dobbs blame corporate greed for many of the job losses. Other critics, including labor unions, say trade agreements are a big part of the problem. They argue that NAFTA cost America more than a million jobs.

Even when jobs stay in the United States, foreign competition exerts downward pressure on wages. Faced with the prospect of losing jobs to foreign competition, workers accept lower wages. With less purchasing power, workers' standard of living suffers. Likewise, unions become more willing to accept job cuts and other terms if a large employer might otherwise go bankrupt. No wonder Alan Tonelson of the U.S. Business & Industry Council complains about a "race to the bottom."

Foreign competition may keep consumer prices lower than they would otherwise be. Yet is it worth saving a couple of dollars here and there if millions of Americans lose their jobs? No way, argues Greg Spotts, author of *CAFTA and Free Trade: What Every American Should Know.* In his view, free trade agreements are just "twisting the knife" in American workers' backs.

Answering the Critics

International trade did not cause all of America's job losses in the last thirty years. Most factory-job losses probably resulted from technological change, argue economists Kent Jones at Babson College and Gary Burtless and others at the Brookings Institution. In one study, Erica Groshen and colleagues at the Federal Reserve Bank of New York reported:

> **[W]hile trade-related competition may have driven job losses in some sectors, layoffs in many other sectors occurred for reasons unrelated to trade. Indeed, in a number of industries, forces such as technological change, investment overhangs [certain funding and investment problems], and changing consumption behavior are much more likely to have caused job losses.**

The story is not all about layoffs, the report added. International trade creates many jobs, and these offset a majority of those that might be lost to imports.

America has also been shifting toward a service-based economy. Providing services is neither better nor worse than manufacturing, argues *The Economist*. Both activities produce income and are often closely linked.

Burtless and his colleagues insist that protectionist policies are not the way to respond to "globaphobia" about open trade. Such a response would likely boomerang and hurt the many American businesses that sell goods and services abroad. Other companies benefit from being able to use imported components or services in making their products. And many Americans, including people with pension funds, benefit from earnings gained through overseas investments.

Beyond this, Burtless and colleagues argue, American consumers enjoy better, cheaper, and more varied products because of the United States' openness to international trade. In contrast, America would suffer from erecting protectionist barriers to trade. Other countries would almost certainly retaliate, as they did during the Depression. Thus, America's export markets would shrink. As Adam Smith argued, government intervention in the form of protection would promote inefficiency. Foreign competition, in contrast, should stimulate innovation.

Lower prices and a greater variety of goods mean better living for American consumers. Economists David Weinstein at Columbia University and Christian Broda at the University of Chicago estimate that the growth in global variety between 1972 and 2001 gave American consumers roughly $260 billion in benefits. One can argue about how various estimates are calculated and whether Americans share benefits from trade equally. Nonetheless, free trade champions say the bottom line is better when consumers enjoy lower prices in the marketplace.

As president of Indus International Inc., Pradip Kamat helps companies form business relationships between North America and Asia. In his view, locating manufacturing and other business activities in Asia makes sense. Billions of people live there, and Americans should be glad that Asian economies are growing.

It is important that not only the 300 million people that live in this country benefit from the economy rising, but also that the remaining 5.7 billion people in the rest of the world start improving their standard of living . . . We benefit dramatically by

**the standard of living in those other countries im-
proving and [their people] being able to afford the
things that we sell.**

In the short term, parts of the economy may lose jobs.
But people need to stay flexible about their career paths
and be open to learning new things. That's true not only in
the United States, says Kamat, but "in any country."

"The higher-end jobs are still here," adds Kamat. "We
are still the most innovative country you can ever find.
And that is what is key."

Innovation is also why free trade critics err when they
assume there are only so many jobs to go around, argues
New York Times columnist Thomas Friedman. There is no
fixed "lump of labor." Thousands of today's jobs in com-
munications, computer technology, and other fields did
not even exist twenty years ago. Global trade helps add
new jobs, often in small companies. News about ten or
twenty new jobs at a time does not get the same headlines
as layoffs of thousands of people. Yet those new jobs add
up, and Americans do benefit from trade.

Yes, it requires a "leap of faith" to trust that there will
be enough jobs for Americans. But Friedman ultimately
sides with Netscape cofounder Marc Andreessen, who
said:

**If you believe human wants and needs are infinite,
then there are infinite jobs to be created, infinite businesses to be started, and infinite jobs to
be done, and the only limiting factor is human
imagination.**

Supporters likewise dismiss critics' arguments about a
"race to the bottom" in worker wages, environmental protection, and other standards. Economist Jagdish Bhagwati
at Columbia University says the evidence doesn't show

Is Science the Answer?

In his 2006 State of the Union address, President George W. Bush announced his American Competitiveness Initiative. In Bush's view, science and technology can keep America ahead in the competitive world market.

> Our greatest advantage in the world has always been our educated, hardworking, ambitious people— and we're going to keep that edge. . . .
>
> First, I propose to double the federal commitment to the most critical basic research programs in the physical sciences over the next ten years. This funding will support the work of America's most creative minds as they explore promising areas such as nanotechnology, supercomputing, and alternative energy sources.
>
> Second, I propose to make permanent the research and development tax credit to encourage bolder private-sector initiatives in technology. . . .
>
> Third, we need to encourage children to take more math and science, and to make sure those courses

are rigorous enough to compete with other nations . . . If we ensure that America's children succeed in life, they will ensure that America succeeds in the world.

Preparing our nation to compete in the world is a goal that all of us can share. . . . [T]ogether we will show the world what the American people can achieve.

Staying ahead in science and technology may be necessary to compete in the world market. But it remains to be seen whether Congress will support the proposed program during the coming decade. Budget battles are an ongoing issue in Congress.

Superior abilities in science and technology will not guarantee jobs for everyone, either. Outsourcing will likely continue. Besides, people in other countries are smart and likewise want to be innovative. In short, building up America's science and technology capabilities is probably a good idea, but it will not end the debate about global trade.

countries competing to attract businesses with low labor or environmental standards. If anything, argue free trade champions, open trade is more likely to lead to a race to the top. Factory workers in Asia and elsewhere will want to improve their standard of living and, as that happens, there will be more demand and more room for everyone in the worldwide job market.

What about the Rest of the World's Workers?

Losing jobs to competition is bad enough when that competition results from real efficiencies in the marketplace. When jobs go to foreign sweatshops, free trade critics object even more vehemently.

Management jobs in shoe manufacturing might pay $80,000 per year in the United States. In Asia they may pay just $36,000 annually, reports Clyde Prestowitz at the Economic Strategy Institute. Line workers may get just $165 to $250 per month. Workers making stereo equipment in China may get just sixty cents per hour for working long days in noisy and dusty workrooms with few safety protections.

When labor is cheap, it is often easier to hire more workers than it is to make expensive capital improvements in factories. However, Prestowitz and other trade policy critics argue, it is wrong to treat cheap foreign labor as if it were a comparative advantage. If anything, America ought to be promoting worker rights worldwide.

The Office of the U.S. Trade Representative is proud of its record negotiating terms to protect labor and the environment. The *2006 Trade Policy Agenda and 2005 Annual Report* prepared by the agency for the President stresses pro-labor provisions in CAFTA and other free trade agreements (FTAs):

WORKERS ASSEMBLE AUTOS AT A BMW PLANT IN RAYONG, THAILAND.

In each of these **FTAs** the parties reaffirm their obligations as **ILO [International Labor Organization]**
members and commit to strive to ensure that core
labor standards, including . . . elimination of the
worst forms of child labor are recognized and protected by domestic labor laws. Each party is also
obligated not to fail to effectively enforce its labor
laws, recognizing the discretion parties have in
matters such as allocation of resources.

Thea Lee at the AFL-CIO feels these FTA provisions are actually a step backward. Instead of giving governments incentives to improve worker conditions in order to get trade preferences, the agreements let countries stay where they are, with inadequate laws and ineffective enforcement. Under some agreements, countries' labor laws could even backslide. Speaking against CAFTA in 2002, Lee argued:

> **Not one Central American country included in the proposed CAFTA comes close to meeting a minimum threshold of respect for the ILO's core labor standards: freedom of association, the right to organize and bargain collectively, and freedom from child labor, forced labor, and discrimination. While the labor movement has been able to pressure Central American governments to improve labor rights with some positive results in a few cases, there are hundreds more where governments have stood by while labor rights are violated, or have themselves been the violators.**

Women and children usually suffer the most, since they have the least political power in low-wage developing countries.

Supporters of trade liberalization policies agree that working conditions in other countries are often below those accepted as standard in the United States or the European Union. However, these are developing countries. As their economic power increases, the argument goes, conditions should improve. Because exporting industries tend to employ more women, argued a study in the WTO's World Trade Review, liberalizing trade should create more jobs for women and raise their wages over time.

NAFTA has increased Mexico's exports and created more factory jobs. However, notes Sarah Anderson at the

Institute for Policy Studies, NAFTA also flooded Mexico with a sea of American-subsidized farm products. Unable to compete, many Mexican farmers moved to the city, causing a glut of workers and keeping factory wages down. NAFTA's weak labor provisions make matters worse, says Anderson:

> **Workers who try to form independent unions in Mexico still face very systematic repression, blacklisting, [and] getting fired for trying to organize a union. It doesn't matter how much they're exporting. If they can't get organized to demand their fair share of the benefits, then it's not going to pay off.**

Georgetown economist Pietra Rivoli notes that today's factories in developing countries share some similarities with American industrial development in the 1800s. In return for toiling up to twelve hours a day, workers at a Chinese T-shirt factory make just $100 or $150 a month. Yet workers told Rivoli they liked their jobs. Factory work was better than the backbreaking, lower-paying farm labor they would otherwise have been doing. Nineteenth-century mill girls in Massachusetts probably felt the same way.

Taking a historical view also suggests worker conditions will improve as more industries offer wider opportunities. China is already experiencing labor shortages in textiles and apparel as workers go to electronics or other industries. "And that itself is causing the conditions to improve, the wages to go up, and so forth," says Rivoli.

Nonetheless, the United States needed lots of social activism before stronger labor laws and union bargaining power led to better working conditions, pay levels, and employee benefits. Unfortunately, China and other countries are not politically accountable to their people in the same way the United States and other democracies are.

And if America's poor people lack political power, that is even more true in many developing countries that have huge gaps between rich and poor.

Fair trade is the best alternative to free trade, argues Global Exchange, a human rights organization. Instead of toiling in sweatshops for the lowest wage the market will allow, workers in fair trade programs get a living wage. They also have a say in how profits are used and employ sustainable methods that protect the environment. Consumers who buy products that are "Fair Trade Certified" know that their dollars are promoting meaningful development.

Fair trade programs are a start, and they are helping thousands of people. Nonetheless, they are only a small part of the world market. Questions remain about how best to help the remaining millions of workers in substandard working conditions. Free market champions say competition will improve things over time. They also question whether the WTO and trade agreements are the proper ways to deal with social issues like labor, the environment, and human rights. In their view, better options would be other diplomatic and international organizations, political processes, and public activism. For example, Nike reformed the labor conditions for producing its brand of shoes and apparel after substantial negative publicity several years ago about foreign sweatshops working under Nike contracts.

Critics feel the present system of WTO agreements and other trade treaties falls short of making sure that the world's people reap the benefits of increased trade. Labor unions and workers need strong legal protection, argues Sarah Anderson: "You can have a better chance of making sure that workers get the benefits of trade if they have strong workers' rights."

6
A Bad Deal for the Planet?

Environmental groups often argue that free trade policies trample over environmental interests. To what extent can and should trade agreements trump other treaties or individual countries' environmental regulations? Environmental activists say our planet suffers while some countries and private parties profit.

Beyond this, many environmentalists feel that free trade contributes to a worldwide "race to the bottom" in regulations. Just as labor critics complain that free trade depresses workers' wages and conditions worldwide, environmental groups worry that free trade fosters pollution and exploitation of limited natural resources.

Free trade champions answer that trade can be safe and environmentally friendly. WTO agreements support countries' authority to adopt and enforce regulations. Supporters say the gains from free trade can also be a powerful incentive for countries to cooperate in promoting sustainable development. As in most matters concerning trade, the debate isn't just about the environment. Countries and commercial interests also stand to win or lose significant amounts of money.

The Trouble with Turtles

During the 1999 demonstrations against the WTO, 240 protesters donned giant turtle costumes and marched into some of Seattle's major intersections. They wanted to publicize the plight of endangered sea turtles caught by shrimpers' nets.

The turtle debate and other complaints involve clashes between countries' positions on conservation and the environment. In general, the WTO tries not to tell individual governments how they must run their nations. The WTO generally does not let any country dictate laws to other nations, either.

However, individual countries have a strong interest in environmental regulation. It does little good to impose costly regulatory requirements on domestic industries if companies can get around them simply by importing from nations with weaker regulatory requirements. Moreover, the environmental consequences of industry and trade do not stop at a country's borders.

Toward this end, Article XX of the WTO's GATT lets member countries take steps to protect health and the environment. However, those provisions cannot be a disguised restriction on trade. Nor may countries apply them in a way that favors their own products or discriminates between countries. Countries argue with each other and before the WTO about just where legitimate protection of health and the environment ends, and where disguised restrictions on trade begin.

The turtle controversy is a good example. Shrimp fishing can kill sea turtles when large trawling nets trap them. In 1998 alone, shrimp nets killed approximately

DEMONSTRATORS DONNED COSTUMES DURING THE **WTO'S 1999** SUMMIT IN SEATTLE. THEY WERE MARCHING TO PROTEST A TRADE DECISION THAT, IN THEIR VIEW, FAILED TO PROTECT ENDANGERED SEA TURTLES.

150,000 endangered sea turtles. Fortunately, fishermen can protect turtles by using turtle-excluder devices that cost about $500.

Since 1989, federal law has said that any shrimp sold in the United States can only be caught using turtle-safe methods. The law applies to all Americans. However, the United States does not catch all the shrimp its people eat. It also imports significant quantities from India, Malaysia, Pakistan, Thailand, and other countries.

A 1994 lawsuit by the Humane Society of the United States, the Sierra Club, the American Society for the Prevention of Cruelty to Animals, and the Georgia Fisherman's Association asked the U.S. Court of International Trade to require that imported shrimp meet the same turtle-safe standards required for domestic shrimp. They won that case in 1996.

Some of the shrimp-exporting countries then turned to the WTO. They argued that the law effectively banned Asian countries' shrimp from the American market. Also, American fishermen had already had time to adapt to the law's requirements. The Asian countries complained that it was unfair to make them meet the same standards immediately.

In 1998, a WTO dispute panel ruled against the United States. The United States could have the turtle-protection provision in its Endangered Species Act. However, the panel ruled, the law acted as an unreasonable and arbitrary barrier to keep Asian shrimp out of American markets. A major factor was the short time allowed before the ban began.

The Sierra Club, Earth First!, the Animal Welfare Institute, the Sea Turtle Restoration Project, and other groups felt outraged. In their view, making money through free trade was no reason to let shrimpers kill sea turtles in their nets. Critics also saw the WTO's action as an attack on individual countries' sovereignty. In their view, the WTO should not elevate commercial interests over the desires of any government or its people to protect the environment.

The WTO has defended its decision. In particular, it said the United States could still protect endangered species.

We have *not* decided that the sovereign nations that are Members of the WTO cannot adopt effective measures to protect endangered species, such as sea turtles. Clearly, they can and should.

The United States lost the case, however, because it discriminated among countries in applying its law. Specifically, the United States assisted Caribbean countries by giving them technical and financial aid, plus more time to comply with the law. India, Malaysia, Pakistan, and Thailand had not gotten those benefits.

Afterward, the United States wound up giving the Asian countries technical and financial help similar to that which they had given other countries. And they allowed time for the countries' fishermen to obtain and begin using turtle-excluder devices.

Free trade champions feel the final result is good for everyone. Sea turtles get greater protection. Asian countries can sell shrimp to the U.S. market. And environmental groups got to voice concerns directly to the WTO when the 1998 dispute panel agreed to allow *amicus curiae* or "friend of the court" briefs.

Tuna, Gasoline, and More

Clashes over environmental regulations and international trade began long before the turtle case and even before the WTO's official beginning in 1995. In one case from the early 1990s, Mexico challenged the United States' ban on tuna that were not caught with dolphin-safe methods. The initial GATT report ruled against the United States, reasoning that the final fish product mattered, and not the way it was caught. Mexico and the United States resolved the issue through independent negotiations—in a dolphin-friendly manner. The resolution came around the same time that the countries were negotiating NAFTA.

In another pre-WTO case, European countries challenged American taxes and regulations aimed at "gas-guzzling" luxury cars. The Europeans argued that the United States' laws effectively worked against imports.

The Americans argued that the laws were a legitimate way to promote energy efficiency. Although its report was not finalized before the WTO officially began, the GATT panel found in favor of the United States.

Soon after the WTO began its formal existence, Venezuela filed a complaint against the United States over its standards for "reformulated" and "conventional" gasoline. Reformulated gasoline had to meet extra standards and was the only type that could be sold in America's most heavily polluted areas. Conventional gasoline could be sold elsewhere, but emissions could be no higher than 1990 levels.

In 1996, the WTO ruled in favor of Venezuela and Brazil, which had joined the case. In environmentalists' view, the WTO was saying that clean air did not matter. From the WTO's perspective, the decision merely said the United States had to use the same standards for both domestic and foreign oil producers. Specifically, the law had let domestic oil producers figure out each refinery's 1990 gasoline emissions on a case-by-case basis. Foreign oil producers could not exceed a level based on the United States average. Thus, conventional gasoline from an outdated, inefficient American plant might be okay. Yet the rule could keep out the same quality of gasoline from another country.

After the WTO decision, the United States negotiated with Venezuela and revised its rule in 1997. The revised rule let foreign producers determine the baseline for gasoline cleanliness on an individual refinery basis. To do that, however, they had to let inspectors from the Environmental Protection Agency into their plant.

For free trade champions, this result shows that countries can negotiate ways to protect the environment while at the same time encouraging international trade. However, environmentalists could argue that the better result would have been to require all producers—both domestic and foreign—to meet stricter standards. Of course, such a rule would have drawn substantial objections from America's domestic petroleum producers.

Timber!

Environmental sustainability is another sensitive issue. Greenpeace and other groups say WTO policies promote greater international trade through plundering our planet's resources. Among other things, WTO policies limit labeling that could let conscientious consumers prefer products made in an environmentally sustainable manner.

For example, a label from the Forest Stewardship Council could assure consumers that wood products came from a "sustainably managed" forest. However, the final wood products would otherwise be the same as competing products. Some countries could therefore complain that the labels are discriminatory under the WTO agreements. Timber operations that clear-cut forests could triumph, while eco-friendly producers would lose whatever advantage labeling could provide. Environmentalists feel this frustrates the goals of sustainable development and limits consumers' ability to choose products that promote conservation.

Meanwhile, government subsidies could make logging more profitable than it would be in a regular competitive situation. That attracts people to the timber industry and spurs clearing of forests faster than they can replenish themselves. The result could be permanent loss of valuable woodlands.

Such subsidies seem to violate the general rules of free trade, since they artificially alter prices and the competitive environment. Yet environmental groups do not all agree that the WTO should resolve the issue. Greenpeace, for example, has argued that timber and fishing subsidies should be dealt with under the Convention on Biological Diversity, which is an environmental treaty, rather than the WTO, which generally has a commercial agenda.

"Frankenfoods"

Traditional breeding methods select strains of plants that yield higher production, survive stress better, or have other useful traits. With genetically modified (GM) crops, scientists actively insert specific genes from other species into a plant to get desired traits and then produce seeds from it. So far, the United States leads the world in developing and growing GM crops.

The Biotechnology Industry Organization and other supporters argue that GM crops are good for the farming industry, the environment, and the world's people. Farmers can often eliminate or use less toxic pesticides and weed killers. Their crops have better yields, which result in lower prices and cheaper food for more people. Future GM crops could offer better nutrition and other benefits too.

Greenpeace, the Union of Concerned Scientists, and other groups have various worries about GM crops disturbing the ecological balance. They also criticize how large companies develop and market crops and seeds. Above all their concerns is fear of the unknown. Critics worry that genetic engineering tampers with nature in a dangerous way.

Like a genie let out of a bottle, GM crops are almost impossible to recall once they get into the general environment. GM crop critics thus argue for the "precautionary principle." Until scientists are certain that a GM crop will never harm health or the environment, critics want to stop the spread of such organisms.

In 1998, the European Union halted approvals on any

new GM crops. The freeze effectively halted further sales of GM seeds and foods to EU countries. Indeed, because most American exporters never separated GM crops from non-GM crops, the freeze kept many American farm products, including most corn, out of the European market. American corn growers lost about $300 million per year in sales.

Then in 2000, representatives of various countries met in Montreal as the United Nations Convention on Biological Diversity. By November 2006, 136 countries (but not the United States) had approved the Cartagena Protocol on Biosafety that resulted from that meeting. The Cartagena Protocol basically adopts the precautionary principle for judging GM crops. Among other things, it lets nations require prior notice and labeling of any imported GM organisms, including seed. Countries can adopt added restrictions too. The European Union's moratorium on GM foods fell into that category.

Under two WTO agreements, however, nations promise not to use safety or environmental standards to block imports unless a science-based risk assessment provides objective reasons for doing so. This approach says that a country should show that a particular import in fact poses a significant risk. In other words, instead of speculating that there might be a risk, a country would have to show it actually exists.

WTO members agree that the trade treaties take precedence over any other agreements. The Cartagena Protocol has some similar language. Other provisions say it does not contradict other treaties.

The European Union ended its widespread freeze by approving a GM corn variety for human food in 2004. However, it let several EU members continue to keep new GM foods out. In 2003, the United States, Argentina, and Canada complained to the WTO.

In 2006, the WTO issued a preliminary ruling against

the European Union. The WTO panel did not say outright that the rules for reviewing the safety of new crops were void per se. However, the European Union apparently did not follow all of its own rules in adopting the moratorium. The dispute panel postponed its final report, pending further submissions from the parties. Controversy over trade in GM crops will likely continue.

Plundering the Planet?

Growth in international trade has led to growth in pollution as well. In richer nations, popular pressure has led governments to adopt ever-stricter laws for protecting the environment. The United States, for example, has extensive federal and state laws dealing with air pollution, wastewater discharges, and solid and hazardous wastes.

Developing countries rarely have regulatory requirements that are as strict as those in wealthier nations. In order to meet basic needs, their leaders often place a higher priority on economic growth than on environmental regulation. Thus, even new industrial plants may not face strict limits on air emissions. Regulatory requirements on wastewater discharges and solid waste disposal are often lax, too.

As manufacturing expands, air and water become polluted. Hazardous waste, mining slag, and other solid wastes wind up buried or littered across the land with little containment or control. Meanwhile, large numbers of people flock to urban centers, working in factories, buying cars, and using electricity. That places added strains on limited resources.

Acting solely in their self-interest, few business owners volunteer to control or clean up pollution. After all, individual factories or other businesses do not bear the costs of pollution. Pietra Rivoli at Georgetown University explains:

Environmental problems are a classic problem that the market cannot solve, because polluters don't pay to pollute. On the other hand, society pays when people pollute. So if we just left it up to the market, all of us would be dumping our garbage everywhere.

Environmental regulations in the United States and other developed nations came about after many people became concerned about pollution. Armed with that knowledge, they pressured elected representatives to act. Awareness about environmental issues will likely increase as other countries' economies grow. However, those countries' governments will not necessarily rush to take action.

Consider the case of China, where the state still owns or controls most industrial operations. "Even if the people are demanding better environmental conditions, they're not necessarily going to get them in China, just because of the lack of accountability in the political system," notes Rivoli.

No wonder, then, that China has become not only a leader in exports, but a leading polluter as well. The World Health Organization reported in 1998 that seven of the world's ten most-polluted cities were in China. By 2004, it had sixteen of the top twenty polluted cities.

China is not the only country where pollution is a big problem. Because of industrialization, an "Asian Brown Cloud" of pollution now hovers over most of South Asia. Nor is that pollution confined to any country's borders. Global currents can carry contaminants around the globe.

Environmentalists say such pollution is not just the fault of the developing countries. They blame multinational companies that buy from or operate in those areas. After all, the companies profit more than anyone else from exploiting the environment.

Indeed, environmentalists argue, companies have an

Friends of Fish

Environmental groups do not always clash with free trade advocates. The two camps came out on the same side in a recent push for stronger rules against fishing subsidies.

Fishing subsidies are payments or other supports by certain governments that increase income or reduce costs for their countries' fishing industries. Subsidies encourage people and companies to stay in the fishing industry and bolster their overall profitability. Several countries in the European Union have been most vigorous in supporting fishing subsidies. Japan and Korea have significant subsidy programs as well. As 2006 began, government subsidies made up about a fifth of worldwide revenues for the fishing industry.

Subsidized fishermen can charge less than nonsubsidized foreign competitors. Subsidies especially disadvantage the fishing industries of poor countries. They cannot match the richer countries' payments to their own fishermen. The domestic fishing industry's catch may not even sell well at home if it must compete with cheaper imports.

Furthermore, subsidies encourage fishermen to fish as much as possible to maximize their government aid. The result is overfishing of the world's oceans. The world's fishing fleet is already two-and-a-half times larger than the size needed to catch the amount of fish the oceans can sustainably produce, reports the World Wildlife Fund. Three-fourths of the world's oceans have already been overfished or fished to their limit.

If fish populations cannot reproduce and maintain themselves, species could become endangered and disappear. Depleted fisheries would also upset the natural food chain in the oceans and hurt other species.

Spurred by these concerns, several countries formed a "Friends of Fish" coalition during the Doha Round of WTO trade negotiations. The group included the United States, along with Australia, Argentina, Chile, Iceland, and other countries. They got the WTO to agree at its 2005 meeting in Hong Kong to adopt stronger rules against fishing subsidies.

Oceana, Defenders of Wildlife, Friends of the Earth, the World Wildlife Fund, and other environmental groups expressed support for the "Friends of Fish" move. And free trade champions like the Office of the U.S. Trade Representative welcomed that support. Both sides anticipate the final rules will be a victory for both free trade and the environment.

incentive to locate industrial operations in countries with lax regulations. Just as labor groups complain that free trade fosters a "race to the bottom" in workers' wages and conditions, environmental groups argue that free trade encourages lax environmental laws.

Supporters of free trade disagree. For one thing, notes the Cato Institute, regulatory requirements to protect the environment are "at best a minor factor" in business decisions about where to locate production facilities. More important factors include how well countries protect foreign investors' property rights, the supply of qualified workers, and the quality of the nation's infrastructure. The infrastructure includes things like transportation systems, available water supplies, and basic health facilities.

Free trade champions also disagree with the notion that businesses have a built-in incentive to pollute. Companies building new plants generally want the most efficient production, regardless of where the plants are. Often that technology produces less pollution than outdated facilities. Companies would also waste resources if they tailored each plant to the least restrictive regulations in each country. Standard production processes lead to cost savings as well. Thus, companies may prefer just to meet the most stringent environmental requirements at all their plants.

Also, as economies grow, environmental conditions tend to improve. People prefer and often demand better and cleaner conditions. When countries move out of "survival mode," they can better afford the costs that come with protecting the environment.

Even China, which is not a democracy, has incentives to act. The pollution caused by its rapid industrialization is affecting its continued economic growth. One World Bank study found that pollution is costing China 8 to 12 percent of its annual GDP, through higher health-care expenses, lost work time from illness, impacts on crops, and depleted resources. As a result, the Chinese government has passed new laws and is adopting new policies through its State Environmental Protection Agency. Yet the country still has a long way to go to clean up its act on the environmental front.

7
Trade and the Future: How Should We Deal with It?

Should the United States and the WTO stay on the current course of promoting trade liberalization? It is unlikely that the United States will withdraw from the arena of international trade. Too many businesses depend on both imports and exports. Similarly, few camps suggest getting rid of the WTO or going back to the widespread tariffs and other trade barriers that prevailed eighty years ago. Yet many people would like to see changes and reforms.

The question then is not, "Deal or no deal?" Nor should the debate end with free trade champions saying, "Just deal with it!" Rather, the United States and the world face significant questions about what directions trade and other economic policies will take in the coming years. Their decisions will affect not only economic growth, but also politics, culture, and social justice.

Adjustments within America

The United States probably will not continue to dominate worldwide trade the way it did fifty years ago. Of course, our economy is constantly changing. With modern technology and the latest phase of globalization,

INDIA HAS A GROWING MIDDLE CLASS, THANKS IN PART TO THE BOOM IN GLOBAL TRADE.

change seems to happen faster than ever. How Americans adapt to such change will decide how they fare in the global marketplace.

Already, the United States labor force is shifting to accommodate some of those changes. Between March 2001 and December 2004, "goods-producing" industries shrank from 18.4 to 16.7 percent of nonfarm jobs in America. Some jobs shifted because firms began contracting with other companies for services, like cleaning and food service. However, America's manufacturing output went down dramatically in various industries. Losses of 2.5 million manufacturing jobs hit the textile, electronics, computer, and machinery industries especially hard.

Meanwhile, jobs in "service-providing" industries grew from 81.6 to 83.3 percent. Employment among health care providers and educational services grew especially fast. "Ambulatory health care" services—health programs not requiring inpatient hospital stays—added over 584,000 jobs.

Critics of trade liberalization complain that the overall quality of any jobs gained is lower than those lost to foreign competition. Lou Dobbs and Clyde Prestowitz warn that employment growth includes many "menial" and "bottom of the scale" jobs. For example, Bureau of Labor Statistics figures predict growing demand for restaurant workers, janitorial workers, and cashiers. If people cannot replace lost jobs with ones that pay as well or better, their standard of living suffers.

In Mark Weisbrot's view, the trade liberalization debate really comes down to a "question of distribution." America's international competition has increased in the last thirty years. However, its effects vary widely. The richest 20 percent of Americans have suffered little or no harm. Meanwhile, other Americans feel their incomes being pushed down. The result, says Weisbrot, is growing income inequality among America's people:

So the pie keeps growing, but it keeps going to a smaller proportion of the population. That's what these policies have done. They're not free trade. They're a limited form of trade liberalization that applies only to those who are relatively without much voice in the political system.

In contrast, he notes, subjecting doctors to much more foreign competition could have saved consumers as much as trade liberalization has. But then the adverse effects would have hit people in higher income brackets more.

Trade liberalization supporters like Thomas Friedman feel optimistic that America will continue to prosper even with growing global trade. The issue goes beyond whether other countries will eventually be as efficient at production as the United States. Even if some of America's industries shift to other countries now, over time it should still emerge with a comparative advantage in some areas. That comparative advantage should make it worthwhile for other nations to import goods and services from us in those fields.

Indeed, the United States has enjoyed mostly steady growth since World War II. Although some sectors have shrunk, others have grown. Pietra Rivoli says such adjustments in the economy are normal:

A lot of our textile jobs, for example, have gone, but a lot of health care jobs have been created. Ideally, that's kind of the way it's supposed to work. But of course, that does require that people are prepared to be flexible, that they're educated and so forth.

For their own economic future, today's teens are well advised to get a college education and to keep adding skills through the years. Competence in science and technology will be necessary for many jobs. Pradip Kamat also urges students to learn foreign languages and to pursue work opportunities that may arise abroad. Such experiences can make dealing in the international marketplace easier. Staying flexible about career paths will also help as the United States continues to adjust to economic change.

The bigger question is what happens to people who do not have the necessary skills to adapt or make career changes. As Rivoli notes:

> **There's very little you can do in the U.S. economy today if you can't read well, write well, and have some basic literacy with math and computers. So I think the people who are left behind are the people really where we've failed them at the educational level.**

America's education system is itself a broad topic for debate. Yet it is a subject that impacts most other social issues in the United States today.

Even for educated workers with good skills, economic displacement can be devastating. In the best of circumstances, finding a new job in the same field can take several months. Training for another field and then finding a good job in that area can take years. In addition to lost income during that period, there is no guarantee that the other field will pay as well as the first one did, or that market conditions will stay stable enough to avoid more switches.

The present system places the burdens of displacement almost entirely on workers. What can be done to alleviate those burdens?

As a practical matter, the United States is unlikely to drop out totally from the free trade movement. Substantially cutting back on imports could help some parts of the economy in the short term. However, other countries would likely retaliate, and export markets could shrink as well. In the meantime, other nations would go on trading among each other. American producers would also have less incentive to be efficient, and consumers would suffer. Overall, the United States would likely be left behind if it tried to close itself off from imports.

As a less drastic measure, the United States might back down somewhat from its current policy agenda. For example, the United States could take a less aggressive approach and refrain from further reductions of its trade barriers. It could even try raising certain tariffs or other trade barriers.

On the plus side, backing away from aggressive tariff reduction would shift the costs of imports to the industries and consumers benefiting from them. On the other hand, free trade champions would condemn such protectionist policies. In their view, America would lose the overall economic benefits that flow from reducing trade barriers.

Protectionist measures might also violate current WTO agreements, plus various trading treaties. Free trade critics resent those treaties as restrictions on America's sovereign right to change economic policies. Nonetheless, other nations would likely take retaliatory action allowed under those agreements. Then, Americans' access to foreign markets would shrink.

What if policy makers did slow down trade liberalization, even knowing the potential costs? If so, they would most likely limit their action to specific industries. Those might be industries relevant to the country's defense, such as energy, metals, or certain technology areas. Or, protectionist measures could focus on industries that affect vocal, well-organized groups with enough political power and allies in Congress. If foreign competitors are in countries with a particularly poor record on human rights, labor, or the environment, chances for action go up. Nevertheless, it is hard to predict whether any particular protectionist measure would pass.

A middle course is to provide better safety nets for America's workforce, as recommended by Boston University's Paul Streeten, Clyde Prestowitz, and others. Such help might provide improved and expanded unemployment benefits, grants or subsidies for education, and public works programs. Health insurance and other programs would help displaced workers too. Under the present system where insurance is primarily provided through employers, continued coverage for laid-off workers is available only for a limited time, if at all. Even then, the cost is more than many families can pay without a full, regular income coming in.

Who would pay for safety net programs? If America as a whole benefits from freer trade, then perhaps funds should come from the general tax base. On the other hand, one could argue that the richest Americans who make millions of dollars each year get a higher share of the benefits from trade than they bear in actual tax burdens. Moreover, many Americans already feel overburdened by taxes and would likely resist moves to raise their tax burdens. Some might also complain that safety net programs expand welfare, even when programs involve job retraining and education.

Broad-based or industry-specific corporate taxes could fund programs for displaced workers. Of course, many industries have strong political ties. Companies would argue that higher corporate taxes could well lead to further offshoring as companies seek better tax treatment abroad. And they would likely pass the cost of higher taxes through to consumers anyway. Thus, even if voters supported the idea, it would face political hurdles.

Another option would be for companies that benefit

from freer global trade to pay voluntarily, through corporate programs or private foundations. So far, however, private companies are not providing the widespread help that would be needed. Nor does the American business sector seem likely to volunteer it any time soon.

Development and Social Justice

What about the economic outlook beyond America's borders? Sadly, statistics show a stark contrast between the world's haves and have-nots. While people in North America and Western Europe enjoy an average of almost fifteen years of formal education, the worldwide average is only about nine years. Life expectancy is approaching eighty years in the world's richest countries, but it is only in the mid-forties in sub-Saharan Africa, where it has gone down since 1990. The number of people living on less than $1 a day has dropped by about 130 million people since 1990. Nonetheless, the World Bank reports, 1.1 billion people in the world still live in extreme poverty. Total world population in 2006 was about 6.5 billion people.

Does trade liberalization help or hurt the world's poor? WTO figures released in 2005 showed that developing countries' share of trade in goods hit a fifty-year peak of 31 percent.

Supachai Panitchpakdi, the WTO's director-general at the time, said:

> **It is through trade that countries can chart a path towards sustainable development and a higher standard of living. While the trend is encouraging, trade expansion is still hampered by barriers, which must be brought down. These barriers exist in all WTO members and are a drag on economic growth.**

Part of the Deal

Much of the debate over free trade pits big corporate interests, on the one hand, against social, labor, and environmental interests on the other. For some companies, however, corporate social responsibility matters very much. Starbucks Coffee Company's C.A.F.E. Practices program is a case in point.

C.A.F.E. stands for Coffee and Farmer Equity. Any sellers wishing to sell "green" coffee to Starbucks must provide independent certification that they meet the program's standards for environmental practices and workers' pay. The program also pays premiums to sellers who exceed its minimum standards.

C.A.F.E. practices grew out of a pilot program that Starbucks began with Conservation International in 1998. "Coffee grows where conservation issues are really important, and there's a threat to biodiversity in these places where coffee is grown as people try to eke out a living," explains Sue Mecklenburg, Starbucks Vice President of Business Practices. As the program got underway in Mexico, it became clear that the farmers' ability to earn a living mattered just as much as environmental practices.

"If you're dealing with agricultural products, sustainability really means that farmers need to be sustainable in their livelihoods in order for you to be sustainable as a business," says

Mecklenburg. "And so it certainly isn't an either/or. We are mutually dependent on each other's successes."

While Starbucks buys only about 2 percent of the world's coffee, the company specializes in high-quality premium coffee. Anecdotal reports suggest the program's practices have helped growers weather storms better and provided other benefits. "And so it made sense to the farmers, it made sense to the company, and it made sense to our customers," says Mecklenburg. She's especially proud of the program's built-in incentives that "pull" good practices through the supply chain.

"What you're trying to do in any of these sustainable systems is set up win/wins," says Mecklenburg. If consumers like the program, that is fine. However, C.A.F.E. Practices do not depend upon consumer response. "We are buying coffee sustainably and having programs in place because it's right for our business," she says. "And they're a good investment in our long-term sustainability."

Look up the practices of the companies you buy from most often. Think about market pressures and other factors that might make similar programs easier or harder for different types of businesses.

The World Bank predicted that 144 million people could escape poverty if the WTO reaches agreement on items from the WTO's Doha Development Round of trade talks. William Cline at the Center for Global Development suggests that those measures and other trade liberalization policies could lift between 400 and 500 million people out of poverty. Thomas Friedman feels that free trade can help millions of people worldwide achieve opportunities previously available only to industrialized nations.

Certainly export markets have helped China, South Korea, and other Asian countries. Although India still has millions of poor people, it now has a growing middle class. The country is "already the fourth largest economy in the world in purchasing power," reported Ambassador Ronen Sen. For him, the issue is not whether India's economy will continue to grow.

"It's a question of when we'll be one of the three largest economies in the world," Sen said. "In a sense we'll be reclaiming our heritage." Average annual income was still just $737 in early 2006. Yet that was a significant increase over years past.

Paul Streeten suggests that while various Asian countries have done well, Africa and most of Latin America have been left behind. Moreover, while northern hemisphere countries have pressed for tariff reductions, many have maintained their own subsidies, other non-tariff trade barriers, and immigration restrictions. In his view, such picking and choosing of policies has slowed growth and contributed to unemployment in various developing countries in the southern hemisphere.

Other critics say the numbers and outlooks offered by Friedman, Cline, and others overstate their case. Reviewing Cline's projections and using World Bank data, Mark Weisbrot says most people lifted above the dollar-a-day line of extreme poverty would still live on less than $2 per day. Also, while total dollar gains may sound substantial, he estimates that trade liberalization policies would increase poor countries' wealth by no more than 0.4 percent of rich countries' GDP. If that is the goal, then foreign aid or other public policies might accomplish that more directly and effectively.

Robin Broad at The American University and her husband John Cavanagh at the Institute for Policy Studies warn against "one-size-fits-all" approaches to international trade and global poverty. China, India, and other Asian nations have increased exports and reduced their numbers of "extreme poor" people. However, they have not necessarily done this through free trade. China, for example, has lifted its own import restrictions very slowly, and it still maintains significant control over currency and other aspects of the country's economy. More importantly for the global poverty debate, the number of "extreme poor" has stayed fairly constant in other parts of the world. Indeed, Africa's numbers of "extreme poor" have actually gone up during the last several decades.

Broad and Cavanagh say other myths muddy the issues too. Technology does not by itself push people up a ladder of development if they lack political power. More aid does not magically solve problems without social reforms. And trade does not necessarily spell economic progress for a country's poor people, unless it comes with other political, cultural, and societal changes.

Much of the debate about global trade is couched as free trade versus protectionism. Yet those are not the only options. Nations, especially developing countries, could tailor policies to develop particular industries. Or, perhaps they might pick and choose among trade terms, based on their individual situations. Thus, some countries might reject foreign-subsidized farm products as competing unfairly with agriculture in their own countries, while others might welcome cheaper food for the people.

Another possibility, suggested by Sarah Anderson at

the Institute for Policy Studies, would be to place conditions on foreign corporations' investments or operations that would produce community benefits. One example would be local content requirements, saying that foreign companies must get a certain percentage of their materials in the host country. Another option would be provisions calling for the creation of a target number of good jobs. WTO agreements and regional trade treaties have not allowed those terms so far, since they act as trade barriers and arguably reduce the potential for profits and growth. However, community benefit provisions could make sure the profits and economic growth actually help people in the area, instead of leaving the country entirely or benefiting just a few wealthy people.

Otherwise, says Anderson, "There's no necessary guarantee that if your exports and your investments increase that average people are going to benefit from it very much." Mexico is a case in point. Although NAFTA had increased exports and foreign investment there, the country has seen a rise in poverty, especially in rural areas. Indeed, unless trade agreements have some restrictions or community benefit provisions, as well as strong labor protections, corporate activity could just lead to the rich getting richer at the expense of the poor. Increasing income disparities could worsen existing social tensions.

Trade is also not the only policy choice for dealing with global poverty. Some countries are so burdened by massive international debt that they keep borrowing to pay interest on outstanding debts and have little, if anything, left over for badly needed social programs. The plight of their people has led U2 singer Bono and other activists to lobby for international debt relief.

Other options include more creative, less traditional ways to promote economic growth in developing nations. Microfinance organizations, for example, make small loans to individuals or groups who otherwise would have trouble getting capital from traditional sources.

In any case, reducing poverty requires political and educational reforms in addition to economic changes. Many countries have tremendous income inequality, so that the majority of people have little political power. Other countries are a far cry from providing the basic rights and opportunities we enjoy in a democracy. As Pietra Rivoli notes:

> **If I got to have a magic wand, I would grant as many people as I could a political voice, and as many people as I could a basic education. With those two things the system is going to be vastly improved, because it's the people without education and without political voice that are always at the worst risk of being exploited.**

None of us has a magic wand. Yet we all have a voice in our political system, and we can speak out on matters we care about.

Learn all you can about global trade, economics, and other issues. Resist the urge to think in terms of good and evil, black and white. Instead, consider the pros and cons of both sides, and try to determine who wins and loses from different policy decisions. Then speak out on issues you believe in. Only by using your political voice can you ensure your own rights in the future, and help others to gain those same rights.

Notes

Chapter 1

p. 7, Christina Sevilla, Deputy Assistant U.S. Trade Representative, e-mail communication to author (April 27, 2006); Robert J. Portman, "United States Trade Policy Agenda" (March 1, 2006), p. 3, www.ustr.gov/assets/Document_Library/Reports_Publications/2006/2006_Trade_Policy_Agenda/asset_upload_file151_9073.pdf (accessed November 15, 2006).

pp. 7–8, Paul Wiseman, "WTO Accord Averts 'Failure,'" *USA Today* (December 19, 2005), p. 1B; Don Lee, "WTO Protests in Hong Kong Turn Violent," *Los Angeles Times* (December 18, 2005), p. A3; see also Donald Greenlees, "Hong Kong Police Sruggle as WTO Protests Turn Nasty," *International Herald Tribune* (December 18, 2005), available online at www.iht.com/articles/2005/12/18/news/protests.php (accessed October 19, 2006).

p. 8, Paul Wiseman, "Deeply Divided Trade Talks Kick Off Today; Protests Anticipated," *USA Today* (December 13, 2005), p. 6B; Bruce Carolan, "Collapse of Trade Talks No Cause for Joy," *Buffalo News* (September 21, 2003), p. H5; Robert Gavin, "A Setback for Global Free Trade," *Boston Globe* (September 16, 2003), p. F1.

p. 8, "WTO Anniversary: A Thousand People in the Street," CNN.com (November 30, 2000), http://archives.cnn.com/2000/NATURE/11/30/wto.anniversary.enn (accessed October 20, 2006).

pp. 8–9, Alex Tizon, "Monday, Nov. 29," *Seattle Times* (December 5, 1999), available online at archives.seattletimes.nwsource.com/cgi-bin/texis.cgi/web/vortex/display?slug=2999667&date=19991205&query=world+trade+organization+1999 (accessed April 17, 2006).

p. 9, Portman, "United States Trade Policy Agenda," p. 2; Office of the United States Trade Representative, *2006 Trade Policy Agenda and 2005 Annual Report of the President of the United States on the Trade Agreements Program* (March 2006), Annex I,www.ustr.gov/assets/Document_Library/Reports_Publications/2006/2006_Trade_Policy_Agenda/asset_upload_file765_9077.pdf (accessed March 31, 2006) [hereafter cited as "*2006 Trade Policy Agenda*"].

p. 9, "Industrial Metamorphosis," *Economist* (October 1, 2005), pp. 69–70; "The Great Jobs Switch," *Economist* (October 1, 2005), pp. 13–16; see also "Counting the Ways," *Economist* (December 26, 1992–January 8, 1993), p. 16; "Numbers Not Worth Crunching," *Economist* (July 28, 1990), pp. 15–16.

pp. 9–10, *2006 Trade Policy Agenda*, Annex I.

p. 11, United States Customs and Border Protection, "U.S. Trade Embargo Against Burma (Update)," September 10, 2003, www.cbp.gov/linkhandler/cgov/import/commercial_enforcement/burma_embargo.ctt/burma_embargo.doc (accessed May 15, 2006).

p. 11, James A. Dorn, "Trade and Human Rights: The Case of China," *The Cato Journal* (Spring/Summer 1996), pp. 77–98, available online at www.cato.org/pubs/journal/cj16n1-5.html (accessed May 15, 2006).

pp. 12–13, White House Office of the Press Secretary, "President Discusses American Competitiveness Agenda in Minnesota" (February 2, 2006), www.whitehouse.gov/news/releases/2006/02/20060202-1.html (accessed February 3, 2006).

p. 14, *See*, e.g., "U.S. Customs and Border Control," www.cbp.gov/xp/cgov/import/textiles_and_quotas/ (accessed May 15, 2006).

p. 14, Jin Wang, "U.S. Trade Relations with Japan" (1996), www.uwsp.edu/business/CWERB/1stQtr96/SpecialReport Qtr1_96.htm (accessed October 13, 2006).

p. 17, Peter Morici, "Bush Administration Capitulates to China in Currency Report" (May 12, 2006), www.rh smith.umd.edu/news/stories/2006/opinion/morici_5.12.06 A.html (accessed November 13, 2006); see also David R. Francis, "Why China's Money Matters to You," *Christian Science Monitor* (May 15, 2006), p. 16.

p. 17, Keith Bradsher, "China's Trade Surplus Sets Another Record," *New York Times* (September 12, 2006), p. C6; Keith Bradsher, "China Lets Currency Rise Past Key Level," *New York Times* (May 16, 2006), p. C1.

p. 17, Jeffrey Sachs, "Democrats Should Back Free Trade," *Wall Street Journal* (December 4, 2001), p. A18; Margot Hornblower, "The Battle in Seattle," CNN.com (November 22, 1999), www.cnn.com/ALLPOLITICS/time/1999/11/22/seattle.battle.html (accessed April 17, 2006).

p. 19, Mehrene Larudee, correspondence with Marilyn Marks, September 11, 2006.

pp. 20–21, Pietra Rivoli, telephone interview with author, April 21, 2006; Pietra Rivoli, *The Travels of a T-Shirt in the Global Economy: An Economist Examines the Markets, Power, and Politics of World Trade* (Hoboken, NJ: John Wiley & Sons, 2005), pp. viii, xiii-xvii, 6–8, 86–94, 121, 199–205, 212–215.

Chapter 2

p. 24, Clyde Prestowitz, *Three Billion New Capitalists: The Great Shift of Wealth and Power to the East* (New York: Basic Books, 2005), p. 8.

p. 24, "A Taste of Adventure," *Economist* (December 19, 1998–January 1, 1999), pp. 51–55.

p. 30, Ha-Joon Chang, *Kicking Away the Ladder* (London: Anthem Press, 2002), p. 29.

p. 30, United States Department of State, "Smoot-Hawley Tariff," www.state.gov/r/pa/ho/time/id/17606.htm (accessed May 4, 2006).

p. 36, Jeffrey Garten, *The Big Ten: The Big Emerging Markets and How They Will Change Our Lives* (New York: Basic-Books, 1997), p. 3.

Chapter 3

p. 39, Adam Smith, *The Wealth of Nations*, quoted in Graham Dunkley, *Free Trade: Myth, Reality and Alternatives* (London & New York: Zed Books, 2004), p. 18.

p. 42, Mehrene Larudee, correspondence with Marilyn Marks, September 11, 2006.

pp. 42–43, Edward M. Scahill, "Did Babe Ruth Have a Comparative Advantage as a Pitcher?" *Journal of Economic Education* (Fall 1990), pp. 402–10.

pp. 43–44, David Ricardo, "On the Principles of Political Economy and Taxation," 3rd ed. (1821), Chapter 22, http://socserv2.socsci.mcmaster.ca/~econ/ugcm/3ll3/ricardo/prin/prin2.txt (accessed May 20, 2006).

p. 48, Philippe Legrain, *Open World: The Truth About Globalization* (Chicago: Ivan R. Dee, 2004), pp. 136–40.

pp. 48–49, Paul A. Samuelson, "Where Ricardo and Mill Rebut and Confirm Arguments of Mainstream Economists Supporting Globalization," *Journal of Economic Perspectives* (Summer 2004), pp. 135–46.

p. 50, International Bank for Reconstruction and Development /The World Bank, *Global Economic Prospects, 2005: Trade, Regionalism, and Development* (Washington, DC: World Bank, 2005), p. xvi.

pp. 50–51, Mark Weisbrot, telephone interview with author, May 22, 2006.

p. 51, Ernest C. Hollings, "We Need Alexander Hamilton," *American Prospect Online* (March 27, 2006), www.prospect.org/web/page.ww?section=root&name=ViewWeb&articleId=11351 (accessed May 27, 2006).

p. 51, Bureau of Economic Analysis, "U.S. International Transactions: Fourth Quarter and Year 2005," press release (March 14, 2006), www.bea.gov/bea/newsrelarchive/2005/trans405.pdf (accessed May 3, 2006).

pp. 51–52, Ricardo, *Principles of Political Economy*, Chapter 19.

p. 52, William Poole, "Does the United States Have a Current Account Deficit Disorder?" (April 10, 2001), http://stlouisfed.org/news/speeches/2001/04_10_01.html(accessed May 3, 2006); see also William Poole, "A Perspective on the Graying Population and Current Account Balances" (March 8, 2005), http://stlouisfed.org/news/speeches/2005/3_08_05.html (accessed May 3, 2006).

Chapter 4

pp. 55–56, World Trade Organization, "Understanding the WTO: Members and Observers" (January, 2007), http://www.wto.org/english/thewto_e/whatis_e/tif_e/org6_e.htm (accessed February 5, 2007); *see also* World Trade Organization, "The 128 Countries That Had Signed GATT by 1994," www.wto.org/English/thewto_e/gattmem_e.htm (accessed March 30, 2006).

p. 57, World Trade Organization, "Understanding the World Trade Organization" (October 2005), p. 105, www.wto.org/english/thewto_e/whatis_e/tif_e/understanding_e.pdf (accessed April 19, 2006).

pp. 57–58, Fiona McGillivray, *Democratizing the World Trade Organization* (Stanford, CA: Stanford University, 2000), pp. 1–2, 4–5.

pp. 58–59, The White House, Office of the Press Secretary, "Remarks by the President in Telephone Interview with *Seattle Post-Intelligencer*, November 30, 1999," press release (December 1, 1999), http://clinton4.nara.gov/WH/New/WTO-Conf-1999/remarks/19991130-1650.html (accessed May 2, 2006).

p. 59, World Trade Organization, "WTO Makes Public All Official GATT Documents" (May 16, 2006), www.wto.org/english/news_e/pres06_e/pr442_e.htm (accessed May 21, 2006).

p. 60, Jin Wang, "U.S. Trade Relations with Japan" (1996), www.uwsp.edu/business/CWERB/1stQtr96/SpecialReportQtr1_96.htm (accessed October 13, 2006).

p. 61, Thomas G. Field Jr., "What Is Intellectual Property?" Department of State (January 2006), http://usinfo.state.gov/products/pubs/intelprp/ (accessed May 27, 2006).

p. 62, Andrew K. Rose, "Does the WTO Make Trade More Stable?" (Cambridge, MA: National Bureau of Economic Research, 2004), pp. 1-2, 13; *see also* Greenpeace International, "WTO—Straitjacket on Right to Say No to GMOs," press release (July 21, 2003), www.greenpeace.org/international/press/releases/wto-straitjacket-on-right (accessed May 27, 2006); *see also* Joan Claybrook, "Speech to the TransAtlantic Consumer Dialogue" (February 10, 2000), www.tacd.org/events/meeting3/claybrook.htm (accessed May 26, 2006).

pp. 62–63, World Trade Organization, "Anti-dumping," www.wto.org/english/tratop_e/adp_e/adp_e.htm (accessed October 13, 2006).

p. 65, International Bank for Reconstruction and Development /The World Bank, *Global Economic Prospects, 2005: Trade, Regionalism, and Development* (Washington, DC: World Bank, 2005), pp. 28–29.

pp. 66, AFL-CIO, "# of Jobs Lost Due to NAFTA (1993–2004)," www.aflcio.org/issues/factsstats/upload/trade.xls (accessed May 19, 2006); Robert E. Scott and David Ratner, "NAFTA's Cautionary Tale: Recent History Suggests CAFTA Could Lead to Further Job Displacement," Economic Policy Institute (July 20, 2005), http://www.epinet .org/content.cfm/ib214 (accessed November 15, 2006).

p. 67, Vladimir N. Pregelj, "Trade Agreements: Procedure for Congressional Approval and Implementation," Congressional Research Service (March 16, 2005), www.opencrs .com/rpts/RL32011_20050316.pdf (accessed May 28, 2006); see also "Office of the United States Trade Representative," undated. www.ustr.gov (accessed May 28, 2006).

p. 67, United States Trade Representative, "Statement of USTR Susan C. Schwab Regarding Entry into Force of the CAFTA-DR for Guatemala" (June 30, 2006), www. ustr.gov/Document_Library/Press_Releases/2006/June/Stat ement_of_USTR_Susan_C_Schwab_Regarding_Entry_Into _Force_of_the_CAFTA-DR_for_Guatemala.html (accessed October 13, 2006).

p. 69, *Europe in Figures—Eurostat Yearbook, 2005* (Luxembourg: Office for Official Publications of the European Communities, 2005), pp. 28–29, 64.

Chapter 5

p. 70, Harold Myerson, "Doing Good Jobs, But Losing Them," *Washington Post* (February 15, 2006), p. A21; Irwin Rovner, "Buy 'American,'" *News & Observer* (Raleigh, NC) (February 13, 2006), p. A10; "Ford Stalls," *Traffic World* (January 30, 2006), p. 6; "Amid Tough News at Ford (30,000 Jobs, 14 Plant Closings) and DaimlerChrisler (6,000 Layoffs Last Week), General Motors Reported a $4.8 Billion Loss for the Fourth Quarter, or $8.45

Per Share," *Brandweek* (January 30, 2006), p. 8; "Ford To Close 14 Plants and . . . ," *Washington Post* (January 29, 2006), p. A3; "Realignment at the Big Three," *Business Week Online* (January 25, 2006) (accessed through Infotrac OneFile, March 28, 2006).

p. 72, Philippe Legrain, *Open World: The Truth About Globalization* (Chicago: Ivan R. Dee, 2004), pp. 136, 139.

p. 72, Lou Dobbs, *Exporting America: Why Corporate Greed Is Shipping American Jobs Overseas* (New York: Warner Books, 2004), pp. 8–14; Alan Tonelson, *The Race to the Bottom: Why a Worldwide Worker Surplus and Uncontrolled Free Trade Are Sinking American Living Standards* (Boulder, CO: Westview Press, 2000), pp. 103, 107–109.

p. 72, Pietra Rivoli, *The Travels of a T-Shirt in the Global Economy: An Economist Examines the Markets, Power, and Politics of World Trade* (Hoboken, NJ: John Wiley & Sons, 2005), p. 100; Dobbs, *Exporting America*, p. 13.

pp. 72–73, Greg Spotts, *CAFTA and Free Trade: What Every American Should Know* (New York: Disinformation, 2005), pp. 9–11; Elizabeth Becker, "Textile Quotas to End Soon, Punishing Carolina Mill Towns," *New York Times* (November 1, 2004), p. C1; Dan Morse, "Throwing in the Towel? Cannon, Fieldcrest, Charisma May Live On as Owner Closes Due to Imports, Slow Sales," *Wall Street Journal* (August 1, 2003), p. B1.

p. 73, Patrick J. Buchanan, *The Great Betrayal* (Boston: Little Brown & Co., 1998), p. 13.

p. 73, Michael Lusztig, *The Limits of Protectionism: Building Coalitions for Free Trade* (Pittsburgh: University of Pittsburgh Press, 2004), p. 2; OnTheIssues.org, "Ross Perot on the Issues," 2004, www.issues2000.org/Ross_Perot.htm# Free_Trade (accessed May 16, 2004).

p. 73, Tonelson, *The Race to the Bottom*, p. 117.

p. 73, Kenneth Naughton and Brad Stone, "Silicon Valley East," *Newsweek* (March 6, 2006), p. 42; Alex McWhirter, "Rush Hour: Bangalore's Hi-tech-fuelled Boom Is Continuing Apace," *Business Traveler Asia-Pacific* (March 2006), p. 42; Clyde Prestowitz, *Three Billion New Capitalists: The Great Shift of Wealth and Power to the East* (New York: Basic Books, 2005), p. 102; Dobbs, *Exporting America*, p. 83.

p. 74, Lee Chipongian, "Poor English Threatens Philippines Outsourcing," *South China Morning Post* (March 22, 2006), Business, p. 11; "Egypt Plots Attack on India To Be 'Call Centre Capital,' *Precision Marketing* (November 11, 2005), p. 3; Tim Rogers, "Outsourcing: Why Latin America Is the New India," *Business 2.0* (August 2005), p. 19; "Call Centres To Quadruple in South Africa," *African Review of Business and Technology* (March 2005), p. 29; "South Africa Topples India in Offshore Call Centre Poll," *Precision Marketing* (December 3, 2004), p. 9.

p. 74, Dobbs, *Exporting America*, p. 34; Daniel W. Drezner, "The Outsourcing Bogeyman," *Foreign Affairs* (May/June 2004), pp. 22–34.

p. 74, Robert E. Scott and David Ratner, "NAFTA's Cautionary Tale: Recent History Suggests CAFTA Could Lead to Further U.S. Jobs Displacement," Economic Policy Institute (July 20, 2005), p. 1, www.epinet.org/issuebriefs/214/ib214.pdf (accessed November 15, 2006); AFL-CIO, "# of Jobs Lost Due to NAFTA (1993–2004)," www.aflcio.org/issues/factsstats/upload/trade.xls (accessed November 15, 2006).

p. 74, Tonelson, *The Race to the Bottom*, pp. 14–15, 37.

pp. 74–75, Greg Spotts, "Kill CAFTA," www.aflcio.org/media center/speakout/greg_spotts.cfm (accessed April 3, 2006); see generally Spotts, *CAFTA and Free Trade.*

p. 75, Kent Jones, *Who's Afraid of the WTO?* (Oxford: Oxford University Press, 2004), pp. 51–55; Gary Burtless et al., *Globaphobia*: Confronting Fears about Open Trade (Washington, DC: Brookings Institution, 1998), p. 85.

p. 75, Erica L. Groshen, Bart Habijn, and Margaret M. McConnell, "U.S. Jobs Gained and Lost through Trade: A Net Measure," *Current Issues in Economics and Finance* (August 2005), pp. 1–7, http://www.newyorkfed.org/research/current_issues/ci11–8.pdf (accessed May 23, 2006).

p. 75, "Industrial Metamorphosis," *Economist* (October 1, 2005), pp. 69–70; "The Great Jobs Switch," *Economist* (October 1, 2005), pp. 13–16; *see also* "Counting the Ways," *Economist* (December 26, 1992–January 8, 1993), p. 16; "Numbers Not Worth Crunching," *Economist* (July 28, 1990), pp. 15–16.

pp. 75–76, Burtless et al., *Globaphobia*, pp. 6–11, 20–21.

p. 76, Christian Broda and David Weinstein, "Are We Underestimating the Gains from Globalization for the United States?" *Current Issues in Economics and Finance* (April 2005), pp. 1–7, http://www.newyorkfed.org/research/cur rent_issues/ci11–4.pdf (accessed May 23, 2006).

pp. 76–77, Pradip Kamat, telephone interview with author, May 22, 2006.

p. 77, Thomas Friedman, *The World Is Flat: A Brief History of the Twenty-First Century* (New York: Farrar, Straus and Giroux, 2005), pp. 227–233, quoting Marc Andreessen at p. 231.

p. 77, 80 Jagdish Bhagwati, *Free Trade Today* (Princeton: Princeton University Press, 2002), pp. 58–59, 87; *see also* Friedman, *The World Is Flat*, p. 233.

p. 78–79, The White House, "State of the Union Address by the President" (January 31, 2006), www.whitehouse.gov/stateoftheunion/2006/index.html (accessed February 3, 2006).

p. 80, Prestowitz, *Three Billion New Capitalists*, pp. 20, 66–69, 76–77, 201.

pp. 81–82, Office of the U.S. Trade Representative, *2006 Trade Policy Agenda and 2005 Annual Report of the President of the United States on the Trade Agreements Program* (March 2006), p. 236, www.ustr.gov/assets/Document_Library/Reports_Publications/2006/2006_Trade_Policy_Agenda/asset_upload_file765_9077.pdf (accessed May 23, 2006).

p. 82, Thea M. Lee, "Comments on the Proposed U.S.-Central America Free Trade Agreement (CAFTA)" (November 19, 2002), www.aflcio.org/mediacenter/prsptm/tm11192002.cfm (accessed May 19, 2006).

p. 82, Hildegunn Kyvik Norda, "The Impact of Trade Liberalization on Women's Job Opportunities and Earnings in Developing Countries," *World Trade Review* (2003), pp. 221–231, available online at www.wto.org/english/forums_e/media_e/xmedia_e/wtr_5e_e.pdf (accessed May 6, 2006).

pp. 82–83, Sarah Anderson, telephone interview with author, May 25, 2006.

p. 83, Pietra Rivoli, Telephone interview with author, April 21, 2006; *see also* Rivoli, *The Travels of a T-Shirt in the Global Economy*, pp. 79–83, 86–93, 99.

p. 84, Global Exchange, "About Fair Trade" (2005), www.globalexchange.org/campaigns/fairtrade/ (accessed

May 23, 2006); Kevin Danaher and Roger Burbach, eds., *Globalize This! The Battle Against the World Trade Organization and Corporate Rule* (Monroe, ME: Common Courage Press, 2000), pp. 189–194, 203–208.

p. 84, Bhagwati, *Free Trade Today*, p. 87; Brink Lindsey and Daniel Griswold, "Trade," in *Cato Handbook on Policy* (December 8, 2004), pp. 639, 643, www.cato.org/pubs /handbook/hb109/hb_109–64.pdf (accessed October 10, 2005); Daniel T. Griswold, "Free-Trade Agreements: Steppingstone to a More Open World," Cato Institute (July 10, 2003), www.freetrade.org/pubs/briefs/tbp-018.pdf (accessed October 10, 2005).

p. 84, Sarah Anderson, telephone interview with author, May 25, 2006.

Chapter 6

p. 86, Janet Thomas, *The Battle in Seattle: The Story Behind and Beyond the WTO Demonstrations* (Golden, CO: Fulcrum Publishing, 2000), pp. 8, 24–28; "WTO Seattle Pictures" (1999), http://greennature.com/gallery/WTO-Seattle-Pictures/turtles (accessed April 24, 2006).

p. 86, World Trade Organization, "Environmental Backgrounder: GATT 1994—Article XX on General Exceptions," www.wto.org/english/tratop_e/envir_e/envir_back grnd_e/c7s3_e.htm (accessed April 24, 2006).

pp. 86–87, Rod Arakaki, "A Perspective on 'The Battle of Seattle'" (December 2, 1999), www.nadir.org/nadir/initiativ /agp/free/seattle/perspective.htm (accessed April 24, 2006).

p. 88, World Trade Organization, WT/DS58/R, "United States—Import Prohibition of Certain Shrimp and Shrimp Products: Report of the Panel," 98–1710 (May 15, 1998) (accessed through docsonline.wto.org on April 24, 2006); see also World Trade Organization, "India Etc. versus US: 'Shrimp-Turtle,' www.wto.org/english/tratop_e/envir_ e/edis08_e.htm (accessed April 28, 2006).

p. 89, Christina Sevilla, Deputy Assistant U.S. Trade Representative, Intergovernmental Affairs and Public Liaison, telephone interview with author, April 27, 2006.

p. 89, World Trade Organization, "Mexico Etc. versus US: Tuna-Dophin," www.wto.org/English/tratop_e/envir_ e/edis04_e.htm (accessed October 13, 2006).

pp. 89–90, World Trade Organization, "EU versus US: Car Taxes," www.wto.org/english/tratop_e/envir_e/edis06_e. htm (accessed May 6, 2006).

p. 90, World Trade Organization, WT/DS2/9, "United States—Standards for Reformulated and Conventional Gasoline," Appellate Body Report and Panel Report (May 20, 1996) (accessed through docsonline.wto.org on April 28, 2006); World Trade Organization, "Venezuela, Brazil Versus United States: Gasoline," www.wto.org/english/tratop_e/envir_e/edis07_e.htm (accessed April 28, 2006); World Trade Organization, "Case Study: The Timetable in Practice," www.wto.org/english/thewto_e/whatis_e/tif_e/disp3_e.htm (accessed April 28, 2006). *See generally* Alejandro Martinez-Zurita et al., "Case Study: EPA Gasoline Standards: Greening the Fuel, or Fueling the Greenback," www.commercialdiplomacy.org/case_study/case_epa_gasoline.html (accessed April 28, 2006).

pp. 91–92, Juergen Knirsch et al., "Deadly Subsidies," Green peace International (March 17, 2006), www.greenpeace.org/raw/content/international/press/reports/deadly-subsidies-2.pdf (accessed April 27, 2006); Greenpeace International, "Threatening the Environment," www.greenpeace.org/international/campaigns/trade-and-the-environment/why-is-the-wto-a-problem/threatening-the-environment (accessed May 21, 2006).

p. 92, Biotechnology Industry Organization, "Background Information," 2006, http://www.bio.org/foodag/background/(accessed April 20, 2006). *See generally* Kathiann M. Kowalski, *The Debate Over Genetically Engineered Foods: Healthy or Harmful?* (Berkeley Heights: Enslow Publishers, 2002), pp. 30–46.

pp. 92–93, Andrew Pollack, "World Trade Agency Rules for U.S. in Biotech Dispute," *New York Times* (February 8, 2006), p. C6.

p. 93, "Cartagena Protocol on Biosafety" (2001–2005), www.biodiv.org/biosafety/default.aspx (accessed November 15, 2006); Secretariat of the Convention on Biological Diversity, United Nations Environment Programme, "Cartagena Protocol on Biosafety: Status of Ratification and Entry into Force" (November 2006), www.biodiv.org/biosafety/signinglist.aspx?sts=rtf&ord=dt (accessed November 15, 2006).

p. 93, Biotechnology Industry Organization, "Biosafety Protocol" (2006), www.bio.org/foodag/background/biosafety.

asp (accessed April 20, 2006); Gilbert R. Winham, "International Regime Conflict in Trade and Environment: The Biosafety Protocol and the WTO," *World Trade Review* (2003), pp. 131–155, available online at www.wto.org/english/forums_e/media_e/xmedia_e/wtr_5b_e.pdf (accessed April 20, 2006).

p. 93, "World Trade Organization Dispute: Background and Perspectives," *International Debates* (March 2006), p. 70; FAS Online, "European Union Moratorium on Biotech Foods" (February 8, 2006), www.fas.usda.gov/itp/wto/eu biotech/index.htm (accessed April 20, 2006).

pp. 93–94, World Trade Organization, "Dispute Settlement: Dispute DS291, European Communities—Measures Affecting the Approval and Marketing of Biotech Products" (February 24, 2006), www.wto.org/english/tratop_e/dispu _e/cases_e/ds291_e.htm (accessed April 20, 2006); *see also* Andrew Pollack, "World Trade Agency Rules for U.S. in Biotech Dispute," *New York Times* (February 8, 2006), p. C6; U.S. Department of Agriculture, "European Union Moratorium on Biotech Foods," FAS Online (February 8, 2006), www.fas.usda.gov/itp/wto/eubiotech/ index.htm (accessed April 20, 2006); *see also* "Greenpeace Dismisses WTO Ruling and Predicts Europe Will Stay Closed to GMOs," press release (February 7, 2006), www.greenpeace.org/international/press/releases/WTO ruling060207 (accessed April 20, 2006).

p. 95, Pietra Rivoli, telephone interview with author, April 21, 2006.

p. 95, "A Great Wall of Waste," *Economist* (August 21, 2004), pp. 55–57; Energy Information Administration, "China: Environmental Issues" (July 2003), www.eia.doe.gov/ emeu/cabs/chinaenv.html (accessed April 27, 2006).

p. 95, Stephen James O'Meara, "That Stinks!" *Odyssey* (April 2006), pp. 6–10.

p. 96–97, World Wildlife Fund, "Fishing Subsidies, Over-Fishing, & the Conservation of Marine Resources" (January 7, 2006),www.panda.org/about_wwf/what_we_do/policy/ trade_and_investment/our_solutions/fishing_subsidies/ in dex.cfm (accessed April 28, 2006); United States Trade Representative, "US Welcomes Environmental Group NGO Support of Stronger WTO Rules on Fisheries Subsi-

dies," press release (December 14, 2005), www.ustr.gov/
Document_Library/Press_Releases/2005/December/US_
Welcomes_Environmental_NGO_Support_of_Stronger_
WTO_Rules_on_Fisheries_Subsidies.html (accessed April
28, 2006).

p. 97, Christina Sevilla, Deputy Assistant U.S. Trade Representative, Intergovernmental Affairs and Public Liaison,
telephone interview with author, April 27, 2006; see also
United States Trade Representative, "US Welcomes Environmental Group NGO Support of Stronger WTO Rules
on Fisheries Subsidies," press release (December 14,
2005), www.ustr.gov/Document_Library/Press_Releases/
2005/December/US_Welcomes_Environmental_NGO_Sup
port_of_Stronger_WTO_Rules_on_Fisheries_Subsidies.
html (accessed April 28, 2006).

p. 98, Cato Institute, "Free Trade FAQs," www.freetrade.org
/faqs/faqs.html (accessed October 10, 2005).

p. 98, "A Great Wall of Waste;" Energy Information Administration, "China: Environmental Issues."

Chapter 7

p. 102, Nell Henderson, "Surviving the Shift: Workers Have
Had To Adapt as Global Trade, Technology Transform the
Nation's Workforce," *Washington Post* (February 3,
2005), p. E1.

p. 102, Clyde Prestowitz, *Three Billion New Capitalists: The
Great Shift of Wealth and Power to the East* (New York:
Basic Books, 2005), pp. 205–07; Lou Dobbs, *Exporting
America: Why Corporate Greed Is Shipping American
Jobs Overseas* (New York: Warner Books, 2004), pp.
105–106.

pp. 102–103, Mark Weisbrot, telephone interview with author,
May 22, 2006; *see also* Mark Weisbrot, "Globalism on the
Ropes," in Robin Broad, ed., *Global Backlash: Citizen Initiatives for a Just World Economy* (Lanham, MD: Rowman & Littlefield Publishers, 2002), pp. 38–41.

p. 103, Thomas Friedman, *The World Is Flat: A Brief History
of the Twenty-First Century* (New York: Farrar, Straus and
Giroux, 2005), pp. 230–33.

p. 103, Pietra Rivoli, telephone interview with author, April
21, 2006.

p. 104, Pradip Kamat, telephone interview with author, May 22, 2006.

p. 104, Pietra Rivoli, telephone interview with author, April 21, 2006.

p. 106, Clyde Prestowitz, *Three Billion New Capitalists*, pp. 263–76; Paul Streeten, *Globalisation: Threat or Opportunity?* (Copenhagen: Copenhagen Business School Press, 2001), pp. 162–63.

p. 107, World Bank, "World Development Indicators 2005," http://devdata.worldbank.org/wdi2005/Section1_1_1.htm (accessed May 7, 2006); see also United Nations Development Programme, *Human Development Report 2005* (Oxford: Oxford University Press, 2005), pp. 19–20, 25, available online at http://hdr.undp.org/reports/global/2005/pdf/HDR05_chapter_4.pdf (accessed May 7, 2006).

p. 107, United States Census Bureau, "World POPClock Projection" (October 12, 2006), www.census.gov/ipc/www/popclockworld.html (accessed October 12, 2006).

p. 107, World Trade Organization, "Developing Countries' Goods Trade Share Surges to 50-year Peak," press release (April 14, 2005), www.wto.org/english/news_e/pres05_e/pr401_e/.pdf (accessed October 11, 2005).

pp. 108–109, Sue Mecklenburg, telephone interview with author, March 28, 2006; *see also* Scientific Certification Systems, "Starbucks C.A.F.E. Practices" (2005), www.scscertified.com/csrpurchasing/starbucks.html (accessed May 8, 2006).

p. 110, William Cline, *Trade Policy and Global Poverty* (Washington, DC: Institute for International Economics, 2004), pp. 263–292.

p. 110, Thomas Friedman, "It's a Flat World After All," *New York Times Magazine* (April 3, 2005), p. 33; Friedman, *The World Is Flat*, pp. 9–11, 97, 185.

p. 110, Ronen Sen, Indian Ambassador to the United States, Comments to Cleveland Council on World Affairs, May 6, 2006 (author in attendance); *see also* Fareed Zakaria, "India Rising," *Newsweek* (March 6, 2006), pp. 32–42; Kenneth Naughton and Brad Stone, "Silicon Valley East," *Newsweek* (March 6, 2006), p. 42.

p. 110, Streeten, *Globalisation: Threat or Opportunity?*, pp. 13, 27, 30, 162.

pp. 110–111, Mark Weisbrot, telephone interview, May 22, 2006; Mark Weisbrot, David Rosnick, and Dean Baker, "Poor Numbers: the Impact of Trade Liberalization on World Poverty," Center for Economic Policy Research (November 18, 2004), www.cepr.net/publications/trade_2004_11.htm (accessed May 19, 2006).

p. 111, Robin Broad and John Cavanagh, "The Hijacking of the Development Debate: Why Jeffrey Sachs and Thomas Friedman Are Wrong," *World Policy Journal* (2007) (draft provided to author, May 2006).

p. 111, *See*, e.g., Dean Baker and Mark Weisbrot, "False Promises on Trade," Common Dreams News Center (July 25, 2003), www.commondreams.org/views03/0725-2.htm (accessed May 26, 2006); *see also* Graham Dunkley, *Free Trade: Myth, Reality and Alternatives* (London & New York: Zed Books, 2004), pp. 8–9, 15–16, 221–222.

pp. 111–112, Sarah Anderson, telephone interview with author, May 25, 2006.

pp. 112–113, "The SEEP Network," www.seepnetwork.org (accessed May 7, 2006).

p. 113, Pietra Rivoli, telephone interview with author, April 21, 2006.

Further Information

Further Reading

Aaronsen, Susan. *Trade Is Everybody's Business*. Alexandria, VA: Close Up Pubs., 1996.

Anderson, Sarah, John Cavanagh, and Thea Lee. *A Field Guide to the Global Economy*. rev. ed. New York: New Press, 2005.

Burgess, John. *World Trade*. Philadelphia: Chelsea House Publishers, 2002.

Dudley, William, ed. *Trade: Opposing Viewpoints*. San Diego: Greenhaven Press, 1991.

Frost, Randall. *The Globalization of Trade*. North Mankato, MN: Smart Apple Media, 2004.

"Globalization: Small World," *Faces*, October 2006.

January, Brendan. *Globalize It!* Brookfield, CT: Twenty-First Century Books, 2003.

Peloso, Jennifer. *Free Trade*. Bronx, NY: H. W. Wilson, 2004.

Organizations and Web Sites

The Brookings Institution
1775 Massachusetts Avenue NW
Washington, DC 20036
(202) 797-6000
http://www.brookings.org

Cato Center for Trade Policy Studies
1000 Massachusetts Avenue NW
Washington, DC 20001
(202) 842-0200
http://www.freetrade.org

Center for Economic and Policy Research
1611 Connecticut Avenue NW, Suite 400
Washington, DC 20009
(202) 293-5380
www.cepr.net

Economic Policy Institute
1660 L Street NW, Suite 1200
Washington, DC 20036
(202) 775-8810
www.epinet.org

Institute for Policy Studies
1112 16th Street NW, Suite 600
Washington, DC 20036
(202) 234-9382
http://www.ips-dc.org/index.htm

Office of the United States Trade Representative
600 17th Street SW
Washington, DC 20508
(202) 395-7360
www.ustr.gov

Progressive Policy Institute
600 Pennsylvania Avenue SE, Suite 400
Washington, DC 20003
(202) 547-0001
www.ppionline.org

Public Citizen
1600 20th Street NW
Washington, DC 20009
(202) 588-1000
http://www.citizen.org/trade

World Trade Organization
Rue de Lausanne 154
CH-1211 Geneva 21, Switzerland
(41-22) 739 51 11
www.wto.org

Bibliography

Bhagwati, Jagdish. *Free Trade Today*. Princeton, NJ: Princeton University Press, 2002.

Broad, Robin, ed. *Global Backlash: Citizen Initiatives for a Just World Economy*. Lanham, MD: Rowman & Littlefield Publishers, Inc., 2002.

Buchanan, Patrick J. *The Great Betrayal: How American Sovereignty and Social Justice Are Being Sacrificed to the Gods of the Global Economy*. New York: Little, Brown & Co., 1998.

Burtless, Gary, et al. *Globaphobia: Confronting Fears about Open Trade*. Washington, DC: Brookings Institution Press, 1998.

Collins, Susan M., and Dani Rodrik, eds. *Brookings Trade Forum: 2000*. Washington, DC: Brookings Institution Press, 2001.

Das, Dilip K. *The Doha Round of Multilateral Trade Negotiations: Arduous Issues and Strategic Negotiations*. New York: Palgrave Macmillan, 2005.

Dávila-Villers, David R. *NAFTA on Second Thought: A Plural Evaluation*. Lanham, MD: University Press of America, Inc., 1998.

Dobbs, Lou. *Exporting America: Why Corporate Greed Is Shipping American Jobs Overseas*. New York: Warner Books, 2004.

Dunkley, Graham. *Free Trade: Myth, Reality and Alternatives*. New York: Zed Books, 2004.

Fishman, Ted C. *China, Inc.: How the Rise of the Next Superpower Challenges America and the World*. Scribner, 2005.

Folsom, Ralph H. *NAFTA in a Nutshell*. St. Paul, MN: West Group, 1999.

Friedman, Thomas L. *The World Is Flat: A Brief History of the Twenty-First Century*. New York: Farrar, Straus and Giroux, 2005.

Gomory, Ralph, and William J. Baumol. *Global Trade and Conflicting National Interests*. Cambridge, MA: MIT Press, 2000.

Ingco, Melinda. *Agriculture and the WTO*. Washington, DC: World Bank, 2004.

International Bank for Reconstruction and Development/The World Bank. *Global Economic Prospects, 2005: Trade, Regionalism, and Development*. Washington, DC: World Bank, 2005.

Jones, Kent. *Who's Afraid of the WTO?* Oxford: Oxford University Press, 2004.

Lechner, Frank J., and John Boli, eds. *The Globalization Reader*. Oxford, UK: Blackwell Publishers, 2000.

Legrain, Philippe. *Open World: The Truth About Globalization*. Chicago: Ivan R. Dee, 2004.

Lusztig, Michael. *The Limits of Protectionism: Building Coalitions for Free Trade*. Pittsburgh: University of Pittsburgh Press, 2004.

Mayer, Frederick W. *Interpreting NAFTA: The Science and Art of Political Analysis*. New York: Columbia University Press, 1998.

McGillivray, Fiona. *Democratizing the World Trade Organization*. Stanford, CA: Hoover Institution on War, Revolution and Peace, 2000.

Moore, Mike. *A World Without Walls: Freedom, Development, Free Trade and Global Governance*. Cambridge: Cambridge University Press, 2003.

Orme, William A. Jr. *Understanding NAFTA: Mexico, Free Trade, and the New North America*. Austin, TX: University of Texas Press, 1996.

Prestowitz, Clyde. *Three Billion New Capitalists*. New York: Basic Books, 2005.

Rivoli, Pietra. *The Travels of a T-Shirt in the Global Economy*. Hoboken, NJ: John Wiley & Sons, 2005.

Rose, Andrew K. *Does the WTO Make Trade More Stable?* Cambridge, MA: National Bureau of Economic Research, Inc., 2004.

Spotts, Greg. *CAFTA and Free Trade: What Every American Should Know*. New York: Disinformation Company Ltd., 2005.

Streeten, Paul. *Globalisation: Threat or Opportunity?* Copenhagen: Copenhagen Business School Press, 2001.

Sutherland, Peter, et al. *The Future of the WTO: Addressing Institutional Challenges in the New Millennium*. Geneva: World Trade Organization, 2004. http://www.wto.org/english/thewto_e/10anniv_e/future_wto_e.pdf (accessed April 19, 2006).

Thomas, Janet. *The Battle in Seattle: The Story Behind and Beyond the WTO Demonstrations*. Golden, CO: Fulcrum Publishing, 2000.

Tonelson, Alan. *The Race to the Bottom*. Boulder, CO: Westview Press, 2000.

Trade & Environment at the WTO. Geneva: World Trade Organization, April 2004. http://www.wto.org/english/tratop_e/envir_e/envir_backgrnd_e/trade_env_e.pdf (accessed April 19, 2006).

Wallach, Lori, and Patrick Woodall. *Whose Trade Organization? A Comprehensive Guide to the WTO*. New York: New Press, 2004.

Index

Page numbers in **boldface** are illustrations, tables, and charts.

social issues, 10–11, 80–84,
101, 111–113
solid waste disposal, 94
South Africa, 36, 74
South American Common
Market, 69
Southern African Customs
Union, 69
South Korea, 35–36, 96, 110
sovereignty, 57, 64–67, 88, 105
Soviet Union, 33, 34–35
Spotts, Greg, 74
standard of living, 34–36,
74, 76, 80, **101**, 102, 107,
110
Starbucks coffee, 108, 109
State Environmental Protection
Agency (China), 99
Streeten, Paul, 106, 110
subsidies, 15, 20–21, 63, 106,
110
as harmful, 91, 96
supply, concept of, 44, 46–47
sweatshops, 80, 84

tariffs, 7, 13, 21, 28–29, 32,
43–44, 47, 65, 100
high, protectionist, 28,
30, 39, 50, 51, 105
reduction, 29, 33, 50, 56,
65–66, 104, 110
retaliatory, 30, 64, 105
tax burden, 106
Tea Act of 1773, 26
Teamsters Union, **68**
technology, effect of, 7, 36,
45–46, 48, 60, 72–73, 77, 78,
79, 100, 104, 111
telecommunication, 7, 36, 48, 74
textile industry, 72–73, 83, 102,
103
Thailand, 72, **81**, 87, 89
timber industry, 91–92
Tonelson, Alan, 74
Torrens, Robert, 41
trade barriers, 7–11, 13, 33, 39,
43–45, 47, 51, 58, 76, 100,
110, 112
in colonial America, 26–28,
27
disguised restrictions, 86, 88,
89–90
lowering, 12, 33, 45, 50, 56,
60, 65–66, 104–105
raising, 61, 64–65, 104–105
trade policy, 10, 12–13, 19, 21,
26–28, **27**, 30–31, 49, 52, 64,
65, 76, 80, 104–105
future directions, 100,
104–105
historic influences on, 38–41
Trade-Related Aspects of
Intellectual Property Rights
(TRIPS), 56, 60, 61
trade routes, 23, 24
transportation, 7, 36, 48, 74, 98
treaties, 63, 65–66, 85, 92–93,
105
community benefit provision,
112
WTO agreements as, 56,
61–62, 84
T-shirt, travels of a, 20–21
Turkey, 36

Union of Concerned Scientists,
92
United Nations, 32, 72, 93
United States, 12, 26–29, **27**,
53, 57–58, 60, 82, 93, 97

About the Author

Kathiann M. Kowalski has written seventeen books and approximately four hundred articles and stories for young people. Her most recent book for Marshall Cavendish was *Affirmative Action*, also in the Open for Debate series. Kowalski received her bachelor's degree in political science from Hofstra University and her law degree from Harvard Law School, where she was an editor of the *Harvard Law Review*. In addition to her writing career, Kowalski has spent fifteen years practicing law and more than ten years writing books. Kowalski's various books have won awards from The Society of School Librarians International, the American Society for the Prevention of Cruelty to Animals, and The Pennsylvania School Librarians Association (PSLA).